Attitudes, Language, and Change

Attitudes, Language, and Change

Anne Ruggles Gere
University of Washington

Eugene Smith
University of Washington

National Council of Teachers of English
1111 Kenyon Road, Urbana, Illinois 61801

Grateful acknowledgement is made for permission to reprint the following material: Jim Quinn's "Plain English," © *The Washington Post Magazine*, 1977. "English Usage Questionnaire" from *Attitudes to English Usage* by W. H. Mittins, Mary Salu, Mary Edminson, and Sheila Coyne, © Oxford University Press, 1970. Reprinted by permission of Oxford University Press. Orlando Taylor, "Teachers' Attitudes toward Black and Nonstandard English as Measured by the Language Attitude Scale," in *Language Attitudes: Current Trends and Prospects*, edited by Roger W. Shuy and Ralph W. Fasold. © Georgetown University, 1973.

NCTE Editorial Board: Thomas J. Creswell, C. Kermeen Fristrom, Rudine Sims, Donald C. Stewart, Ann Terry, Robert Hogan, *ex officio*, Paul O'Dea, *ex officio*

Book Design: Tom Kovacs

NCTE Stock Number 02174

© 1979 by the National Council of Teachers of English. All rights reserved. Printed in the United States of America.

It is the policy of NCTE in its journals and other publications to provide a forum for the open discussion of ideas concerning the content and the teaching of English and the language arts. Publicity accorded to any particular point of view does not imply endorsement by the Executive Committee, the Board of Directors, or the membership at large, except in announcements of policy where such endorsement is clearly specified.

Library of Congress Cataloging in Publication Data

Gere, Anne Ruggles, 1944-
   Attitudes, language, and change.

   Bibliography: p.
   1. English language—Study and teaching.
2. English language—Social aspects.
3. Linguistic change.   4. Attitude (Psychology)
I. Smith, Eugene, 1927-   joint author.
II. Title.
PE1065.G46   301.2'1   79-20099
ISBN 0-8141-0217-4

```
PE 1065 .G46
Gere, Anne Ruggles, 1944-
Attitudes, language, and
  change
```

With thanks to Marcia and Budge, our spouses, for their trust and support.

Contents

Preface ix

1. Conflicts in Attitudes toward Language 3
2. Language Attitudes and the Change Process 17
3. Changing Language Attitudes within the Profession 41
4. Changing Language Attitudes in the Community 61

Appendix 79
Bibliography 105

Preface

As a teacher of English perhaps you share our concern with language usage. Shall we frown at "hopefully"? Is "drapes" an acceptable substitute for "draperies"? What about "daylight savings time"? Must "good English" be the same set of forms and conventions for all occasions? Like us, you may have been asked to help establish linguistic shibboleths of inclusion or exclusion, and you may have felt the tension of negotiating between public expectations and linguistic training.

Teaching at elementary, secondary, and university levels, we have participated in many conversations about language. We have heard recurrent patterns of questions and unresolved responses: groups of teachers sharing their concerns about improving students' language, about searching for defensible language standards, about the possible use of new linguistic knowledge, about feeling community pressures to maintain the precedents of old-fashioned grammar. Few of these conversations addressed attitudes about language itself and fewer still have considered the relationship between attitudes and usage.

We believe that examination of attitudes is part of our urgent business as English teachers, that the route to better language teaching lies in serious attention to attitudes. What do we and our colleagues believe about language? How can we scrutinize these attitudes? Should we change any of our attitudes toward language?

We cannot offer simple methods for approaching language attitudes or for changing them. But if we English teachers begin to talk about feelings toward as well as knowledge of language, we may find answers to some of our concerns. This book suggests ways of beginning the dialogue.

Characters: Sue Carlucci, Frank Burr, and Liz Schutz, English teachers
              Joe Motz, history teacher
              Ellen Brown, chemistry teacher
              (These five have the same planning period and meet almost daily in the lounge.)

Scene: A teachers' lounge in mid-October. A sagging sofa and three wicker chairs surround a cluttered work table.

Burr *(throwing his pen down in exasperation):* I quit! I'm not going to circle "it's" one more time. When will these kids learn the difference between a possessive and a contraction? I guess I'll have to get the grammar handbooks out and have the kids work on some exercises.

Schutz: Do you really think that will make a difference in their writing? Everything I've read says it won't; they may even learn to *hate* English. Recently I've tried to point out the good things in my kids' papers and pay attention to their ideas.

Brown: But how can they express ideas if they can't use the English language? Your students need a good dose of old fashioned English, the kind I studied. I remember doing lots of grammar exercises, learning rules—it really taught me a lot. I had one teacher who memorized our grammar book and wrote the page number of the rule beside each error in our writing; then we'd have to look up the rule and copy it five times.

Carlucci: Is that why you decided to major in chemistry? *(Laughter)* Seriously, though, I wonder what you did learn from all that. I'm not comfortable ignoring errors, but I know that my red marks don't change student writing a bit. In fact, . . . *(bell rings)*

Scene: Same place, same group, different day

Carlucci *(looking up from the book she is reading):* Liz, this book you gave me is something else. Listen to this: Robert Hall says "good language is language which gets the desired effect with the least friction and difficulty for its user. That means, of course, that 'good' language is going to vary with the situation it is used in." He gives the example that "he doesn't" would get the best results in one situation, but "he don't" would be more effective in another.

Burr: Does that mean we should say "I ain't got none" because some of our students do?

Motz: Yeah, I thought you English teachers were supposed to uphold the standards, not degrade language.

Schutz: Wait a minute. I've studied English nearly all my life, and I can't tell you what "correct language" is. Look at the usage notations in some of the new dictionaries—48% of the usage panel disapproves and 52% approves; am I supposed to use the word or not? Who can say . . . ? *(bell rings)*

1 Conflicts in Attitudes toward Language

"What attitudes do you have toward language?"
"Huh? Whadya mean, attitudes? Language *is*. It exists. What is there to have an attitude about?"
"Well, how do you feel about people who say 'ain't' and 'don't hardly'?"
"They're the salt of the earth! They don't talk fancy; they just say what they mean."

Most people don't realize that they have attitudes toward language until they are forced to confront or articulate them in some way. Chances for verbalizing these attitudes are rare, so the forces influencing them are covert and powerful. Our professed attitudes may appear enlightened, but they often differ from the subconscious attitudes which inevitably govern our judgments and behavior. Several studies acknowledging this phenomenon have begun to sort out the complex relationships among race, dialectical characteristics, and physical appearance.

In one study, 422 teachers from a nationwide sample responded on a positive-negative scale to a list of statements about nonstandard and Black English.[1] Statements fell into these categories: structure of Black English, consequences of use and acceptance of BE, philosophies concerning use of BE, and cognitive and intellectual abilities of BE speakers. Teachers responded to such assertions as, "Black English is an inferior language system" and "Widespread acceptance of Black English is imperative." The overall conclusion was that the majority of teachers hold positive to neutral opinions, suggesting that a considerable proportion of American teachers, when asked directly, believe language variation is desirable.

Another study, however, which presented teachers and student teachers with children's speech samples and videotapes of the speakers, reports a widespread tendency among teachers to rely on stereotypes in evaluating the speech of an ethnic group as either standard or nonstandard on the one hand and in judging the speaker as confident or nonconfident on the other.[2] In other words, when confronted by actual speech and speakers, teachers may be more heavily influenced by stereotyped attitudes than they realize. This conclusion is supported by a study of fifty students in the Harvard Graduate School of Education.[3] Subjects listened to tape recordings of adult speakers from six dialect groups (such as radio announcers, college-educated white southerners, and southern black students from a small all-black Mississippi college), and rated each speaker on character traits (friendly, ambitious, honest, and so forth). "Network speakers" ranked highest and the Mississippi students lowest. The study indicates that the listeners' ratings of character traits are affected by how they perceive the race of the speaker. "The simple fact is that people will judge differentially on the basis of certain cues—in this case speech alone—because of their experience and certain, albeit inaccurate, stereotypes."[4]

Stereotypes often dominate our attitudes toward our own speech, as well as that of others. Consider the linguistic self-hatred evident in the New York City speakers studied by Labov.[5] New Yorkers say of their own speech: "It's terrible." "Distorted." "Terribly careless." "Sloppy." "It's horrible." "Lou-say." Referring to New York as "a great sink of negative prestige," Labov observed, "More than half of the respondents thought poorly of their own speech, and two thirds had attempted to change their speech in some way or another."[6] Yet children who move to the city from other regions feel enormous pressure to adopt the local speech pattern:

> The pressure is greatest against those who would attempt to use an acquired prestige pattern too early. A teacher who conducted a class of gifted children told me: "I had a boy of Greek parentage, and oh! he spoke beautifully in class, and I happened to hear him on the street one day. He sounded just like everybody else in Chelsea, and when I mentioned it to him—the next day—he said that he knew which was correct, but he said: 'I couldn't live here and talk like that.'" One of the reasons for the resistance of children to middle-class norm is that their teachers advocate a language, and an attitude towards language, which is quite remote from everyday life.[7]

On the premise that these attitudes often cause confusion, self-delusion, and injustice, we seek in this book to examine the nature of linguistic attitudes and the processes whereby they may be changed. This is an audacious purpose because these attitudes are enormously complex, differing in some respects for every person, and also because the attitudes and the processes of change involve not only intellect but emotion. While it may be foolish to prescribe change in basic attitudes toward language, it is irresponsible not to present reasonable alternatives to fixed notions.

Typical Language Attitudes

Many Americans believe there is a clear distinction between correct English and substandard English, and they believe that school is the proper place to teach and enforce that distinction. But such a rigid attitude is difficult to maintain in schools because teachers do not readily align themselves with so monolithic an attitude. James Sledd has pinpointed the seven most common teacher attitudes toward usage:

> The first denies all standards; it assumes that whatever a person says is right for him. The second does not question either, but it relies on an observance of rules. They are simply to be obeyed, not to be reasoned about. The third is the standard of "unrationalized taste." Let your feelings be your guide and cultivate those feelings in others. The fourth, which appeals to the "factual minded," turns to prestige dialect for its standard. "Whatever is in the language of the chosen people must be right." The fifth reveres the tradition of the past. It wants only to preserve useful distinctions and to retard linguistic change. The sixth is committed to social mobility; it encourages the usage that will enable the student to rise in the world. The last is the one that surmounts these confusions and narrow loyalties. It can only commit itself completely, from one paper to the next, to the particular fitness of means and end, the appropriateness of the language to the writer's specific purpose.[8]

If the range of language attitudes among teachers is greater than that of the public, as Sledd suggests, we must conclude that many teachers have at least begun the difficult process of detaching themselves from prevailing views. Such detachment is difficult because teachers, after all, share the preconceptions of the general public, even though, as professionals, they are obliged to bring the study and use of language to an analytical level.

Language Attitudes in Context

Attitudes toward language are part of the larger framework of language which determines our view of both the physical environment—objective reality—and the structure of our internal existence—subjective reality. The Sapir-Whorf hypothesis presents the rather extreme view that language drastically and inevitably shapes thought by categorizing the world—into colors, plants, precipitation, food, clothing, time, etc. We rely on these categories to consider, communicate, and interpret our experiences. Therefore, according to Sapir-Whorf, our psychological bearings are formed and regulated by our native language.[9] Our own feeling, however, as students and teachers of English, is that there is not enough empirical evidence to support so extreme a view. We see language as a medium, not a legislator.

A more moderate version of the Sapir-Whorf hypothesis has been formulated by several psychologists, among them Jerome Bruner, whose book, *On Knowing: Essays for the Left Hand*, offers provocative insights into our ways of knowing the world. Bruner suggests that instead of "ineluctably" shaping thought, "language predisposes a mind to certain modes of thought and certain ways of arranging the shared subjective reality of a linguistic community."[10] "Predisposing" means creating probable shapes, patterns, and networks without forcibly preventing others. Word and sentence meanings are the products of reasoning, or, to use Bruner's metaphor, "right-handed" meanings. (Readers who are familiar with recent studies of brain function will recognize that "right-handed" functioning corresponds to the left hemisphere of the brain; "left-handed" functioning is controlled by the right hemisphere of the brain.)

Our "left-handed" way of knowing the world and sharing the meanings we discover in it draws upon another part of our internal existence. Rich in emotional content and created partly from the nonrational dimensions of experience, these meanings take shape as myths. "Myth" used in this sense may or may not be externally provable "truth." The point is that myths contain a subjective reality—feelings, beliefs, and values—that helps us comprehend the external world and form a basis for behavior. Their effect is circular because while the myths "instruct" the community in values, behavior, and goals, they also supply the criteria for judging our progress. Bruner sees each of us as "multiple identities" following a constantly rewritten script with a constantly rotating cast.[11] The myths filter our external experiences, controlling and synthesizing our intake of data to avoid internal chaos.[12] These myths often have a strong central image. In America, the Horatio Alger myth, the frontier myth, and the progress myth are influential and widespread examples. The Horatio Alger stories draw upon the desire to rise from obscurity to wealth and prominence through native wit and hard work. The notion that there are literal and figurative frontiers in all the major fields of human achievement combines the need for challenge and excitement with a definite goal. And a belief that individually and collectively we are engaged in the overall improvement of human life makes progress seem real and provides a standard for measuring our efforts. Circularity is complete when the myths that we create become shapers of our creative process.

We are suggesting, then, that language and myth are very powerful determiners of behavior and that the attitudes we hold are shaped by both. The evolution of acculturating myths was not a willed and wholly conscious process for any of us, but was the result of our deep-seated needs and values. Obviously, trying to *change* an attitude based on commonly accepted myths is quite different from *acquiring* such an attitude. No one sets out to teach us most attitudes; we simply absorb them as part of our normal growth. If, at some time in our lives, we feel we must change an attitude, it is a conscious effort to modify our thinking and, indirectly, the premise of a deeply rooted myth. Our defenses against change are strong because they are steeped not only in objective reality, which is approached by logic, but also in subjective reality, which is either inaccessible to logical reasoning or is only indirectly affected by it. Sometimes even the most outrageous myths, such as those centering on the superiority of certain races, can be supported by reasoning which seems logical, given certain premises. These myths are often the most deep-seated, and are therefore the most difficult for ourselves or others to change. Against a critical world, we must each create a fortress for ourselves, a stronghold we wish not to alter without strong reason to do so.

Some Influential Language Myths

The origins of many myths about language are difficult to trace. One exception, which became popular in the 1960s, is that children who grow up in urban ghettos are verbally deprived when they come to school. This myth developed as educational psychologists presented evidence seeming to show that ghetto children, usually black, produced markedly less fluent language in clinical observation situations than did nonghetto children of the same ages; that this language differed in several structural ways from the language of the adult observers and of white, middle-class children; and that ghetto children seemed to have illogical or distorted concepts about objects and physical relationships. Furthermore, their scores on IQ tests and other measures of verbal performance used by conventional schools were consistently lower than those of white, middle-class children. Using verbal deprivation as a premise, one investigator concluded that one race must be genetically inferior to the other—that the intelligence of black people, and therefore their skill with language, could never equal that of whites.[13] Bereiter and Engelmann, on the other hand, decided that elaborate programs for teaching a first language could help verbally deprived children to acquire what "normal" children already possessed.[14]

What these educational psychologists failed to examine was the actual language of these "verbally deprived" children. William Labov, a linguist, did examine it and discovered that the very same kinds of children whom other scientists pronounced deprived actually have a language every bit as complex, flexible, and powerful for communication as speakers of standard English. Labov concludes:

> Negro children in the urban ghettos receive a great deal of verbal stimulation, hear more well-formed sentences than middle-class children, and participate fully in a highly verbal culture. They have the same basic vocabulary, possess the same capacity for conceptual learning, and use the same logic as anyone else who learns to speak and understand English.[15]

Labov's observations lead to a myth of verbal parity, not one of verbal deprivation. However, scientific evidence alone is usually not persuasive enough to supplant a prevailing myth, and most of us choose the version we want to believe by fitting the "scientific facts" into an existing framework of attitudes.

This same process of myth-making and choice applies to "standard English." Because the word *standard* implies some fixed criteria for comparison, the phrase can be used only with certain assumed points of reference which may be cultural or linguistic. We have formulated the following pairs of statements that suggest contrasting premises about the users of English and about the linguistic integrity of their choices. In each case, the premises and conclusions which together constitute the myth exist within a larger context of values and beliefs.

Myth 1a: Some people, such as blacks and hillbillies, speak a version of English that is degenerate. Signs of this degeneracy can be found in their sloppy pronunciation, their imprecise vocabulary, and their violation of many grammatical rules. All of these signs point to a form of language which is inadequate for accurate communication.

Myth 1b: All natural languages and their inevitable varieties (i.e., their dialects) are legitimate forms of human language and equally valid instruments of human communication; none can be shown to be a decayed or degenerate version of another.

Myth 2a: "Standard English" is the kind of language which people *should* use for all occasions. "Standard" means most serviceable and negotiable and therefore most correct.

Myth 2b: "Standard English," particularly in its spoken version, bends as much as any other dialect of English in serving communication needs. The language typically spoken by radio and television announcers is not an adequate model for "standard English." A better model is the dialect spoken by socially and politically prominent people in various regions of the United States.

Myth 3a: "Standard English" is a clearly definable set of correct pronunciations, grammatical structures, and word choices. It is "standard" because it represents the widest usage and because it has been refined to be the most versatile and acceptable form of English.

Myth 3b: "Standard English" in its spoken form is whatever variety of English is currently associated with prestige in a given community. There is much more variation in the acceptable and prestigious spoken forms within "standard" than members of any one community might acknowledge. "Standard English" in its written form, however, has a much narrower range of acceptable and prestigious choices.

Myth 4a: "Standard English" is necessary for success in school and therefore in employment. One of the principal reasons for having schools is to equip young people with the skills necessary to improve their chances for social and financial rewards. Conformity to certain ways of using language obviously underlies several of those skills.

Myth 4b: Some aspects of one's use of language *are* commonly used to indicate one's desire to fit the requirements of a given social situation. Whether or not this is fair is another issue, but given this situation, a decision to use "standard English" should be a voluntary choice of the individual and not a criterion of intellectual or academic aptitude.

Myth 5a: "Standard English" is the best version of English for the expression of logical and abstract thought. Because all of the great English and American writers use this form of English and because much of the business of our society is conducted with this form, it must be the form best suited to the expression of precise and sophisticated thought.

Myth 5b: Logic is not a property of language but of thought, and all natural languages and variations, such as "nonstandard" dialects, have equal potential for expressing thought with clarity and precision.

Myth and Metaphor

The five contrasting assumptions above represent one way of defining our beliefs about language. Another way is by metaphor. As Susanne Langer points out:

> One might say that, if ritual is the cradle of language, metaphor is the law of its life. It is the force that makes it essentially *relational*, intellectual, forever showing up new, abstractable *forms* in reality, forever laying down a deposit of old, abstracted concepts in an increasing treasure of general words.[16]

Metaphors are our habitual way of conceptualizing the world and of talking about it to each other. As such, they are a necessary and desirable medium for much of our thought. But metaphors can constrain thought and even replace it. They can create a self-contained system or context from which it is difficult to escape. Once one metaphorical way of interpreting experiences becomes habitual, adopting another is extraordinarily difficult, and without conscious effort we may resist changing it. Certainly this resistance can and does happen with respect to language itself. Our accumulation of beliefs about language—its structure, its stability, its uses—is often encapsulated in a metaphor which effectively guides our judgments about language. If nothing comes along to challenge that metaphor and if we do not become sufficiently conscious of its constraints, we are not likely to realize its limitations and distortions.

In the story that follows, we have created a character whose reactions to imprisoning metaphors are immediate. Ad-libbing his way through most linguistic situations, the central character is delightfully sensitive to metaphor, and his playful attitude toward language suggests a productive model. Perhaps his exaggerated reactions to the metaphors that control attitude can increase our awareness of their presence and effect.

Restrung Metaphors

Adli Bitum was a curious fellow—always stumbling over old metaphors and wondering what congeries of circumstance had spawned them. Not given to ordinary restraint and disinclined toward scholarship, he poked among the detritus of everyday speech, asked naive-sounding questions, and generally upset the people he met who would rather not have had to explain.

Yet he often came up with some bit of information or a question that revealed worlds of submerged meaning. Even if he himself didn't always realize the significance of his discoveries, just being near him was often to experience an epiphany.

Take the time when Adli, in his usual freestyle manner, took on The Dike Metaphor. Dikes are erected to keep something out, usually a sea or a river reaching floodstage. But dikes are also metaphorically erected to protect a person or a group from inundations of equally distressing bad language—usages such as "like I say," "finalize the plans," and "a most unique experience." Recognizing the engineer's impulse in efforts to protect the public from such pernicious usages, Adli sought out a resident engineer. He found one at the local newspaper office: the copy editor, a green-eyeshaded curmudgeon whose fame with the blue pencil was wide. Stan Dards was his name.

"Tell me, Stan," said Adli, "is your job getting any easier these days? Are young graduates of journalism schools better than they used to be?"

"You'll be sorry you got me going on that subject, my boy. Why, I tell you the world is going to hell in a handbasket. My job is fifty percent harder now, just correcting all their errors in grammar. Can't punctuate. Can't spell. Don't know the fine points of noun and verb usage. Write fragments and use pronouns that have unclear antecedents. It's as though they didn't know handbooks of correct usage exist."

"A real flood of mistakes, eh?" said Adli, putting a finer point on the metaphor that he sniffed.

"That's right. And by damn it's time we put a stop to that flood. What we need in schools is some no-nonsense discipline with language—clearly and consistently enforced standards," said Stan, becoming flushed about the ears. "We must hold the line against further corruption of the language. If we don't, I foresee the demise of literacy and maybe even western civilization as we have known it."

Feeling the chill of apocalypse, Adli retreated to safer ground, the large room where all the young reporters, lodged in cubicles, committed the linguistic atrocities that Mr. Dards so forcefully rejected. A cacaphony of words washed over him as he walked among the intricate pattern of partitions, electrical cords, and telephone gear. Telephone conversations, typewriter tappings, and television and radio monologues blended into an incomprehensible blur.

Adli contemplated all of this with a momentary detachment and suddenly blurted out, to no one in particular, "Lattice. Why not a lattice instead of a dike? Old Stan as good as admits that the dike isn't working. It crumbled long ago, if it ever really stood, and what he sees is pollution seeping in everywhere. Well, maybe we do need some kind of protection from the unregulated flood of language, but wouldn't a lattice serve? It's made with some kind of a design, like this reporters' lair, and it regulates the flow of air, or water, or any other medium to which it is suited. There must be some kind of language lattice that could replace the dike, something that won't let everything in, but something a little more adjustable to occasion than Stan Dards."

Adli had had an epiphany. . . .

Changing Metaphors and Myths

There is something to be learned from our unlikely Mr. Bitum. Incapable of being imprisoned by a metaphor, he possesses a remarkable ability to transform images. When we create metaphors, we demonstrate this ability. Our challenge is to cultivate it, to become more sensitive to the metaphors that we use habitually and that reflect the myths that dictate our attitudes. If we can recognize these myths, we can examine, analyze, and broaden our attitudes toward language. Through constant questioning, we may discover that certain linguistic metaphors and the subtleties of language are incompatible. A common example is the tool metaphor. Language, and written language in particular, is often viewed as a tool. But a tool is external to the user and usually has limited use. To consider writing a tool is to oversimplify its functions and to misrepresent the psychological processes which produce it.

Adli's sudden insight and his ability to form new metaphors are uncharacteristic of most people. Instead, we should expect new metaphors to take shape slowly and to win acceptance gradually. Myths influenced by nonrational forces are part of our emotional structure and are therefore protected from sudden assault. But by consciously seeking to merge our increasing knowledge of language into new metaphors, we may accomplish over time what Adli accomplished in a moment.

Notes

1. Orlando J. Taylor, "Teachers' Attitudes toward Black and Nonstandard English as Measured by the Language Attitude Scale," in *Language Attitudes*, ed. Roger W. Shuy and Ralph W. Fasold, pp. 174-201.

2. Frederick Williams, "Some Research Notes on Dialect Attitudes and Stereotypes," in Shuy and Fasold, pp. 113-28.

3. Bruce Fraser, "Some 'Unexpected' Reactions to Various American-English Dialects," in Shuy and Fasold, pp. 28-35.

4. Ibid., p. 35.

5. William Labov, *The Social Stratification of English in New York City* (Washington, D.C.: Center for Applied Linguistics, 1966), excerpted in *Varieties of Present-Day English*, ed. Richard W. Bailey and Jay L. Robinson, pp. 274-91.

6. Ibid., p. 282.

7. Ibid., p. 284.

8. James Sledd, as quoted by Miriam B. Goldstein, *The Teaching of Language in Our Schools* (New York: Macmillan Co., 1966), pp. 158-9.

9. John B. Carroll, ed., *Language, Thought and Reality: Selected Writings of Benjamin Lee Whorf* (Cambridge, Mass.: MIT Press, 1956).

10. Jerome Bruner, *On Knowing: Essays for the Left Hand* (Cambridge, Mass.: Harvard University Press, Belknap Press, 1962), p. 137.

11. Ibid., p. 36.

12. Ibid., p. 29.

13. Arthur Jensen, "How Much Can We Boost IQ and Scholastic Achievement?" *Harvard Educational Review*, Winter 1969, pp. 1-123.

14. Carl Bereiter and S. Englemann, *Teaching Disadvantaged Children in the Preschool* (Englewood Cliffs, N.J.: Prentice-Hall, 1966).

15. William Labov, "The Logic of Nonstandard English," in *Report of the Twentieth Annual Round Table Meeting on Linguistics and Language Studies*, ed. James E. Alatis (Washington, D.C.: Georgetown University Press, 1970), reprinted in *Varieties of Present-Day English*, ed. Richard W. Bailey and Jay L. Robinson, p. 320.

16. Susanne K. Langer, *Philosophy in a New Key* (New York: New American Library, Mentor Books, 1951), p. 125.

Scene: Same place, same group, different day

Carlucci: You know, I'm beginning to wonder if continuing education is such a good idea. The thing I'm learning from my linguistics class is that I've been doing everything wrong for years. For this I should spend money and time?

Motz: What are you doing wrong? Your classes seem fine to me. Why, you hardly ever yell at the kids.

Carlucci: It's not the way I teach, it's what I teach that's the problem. I've always thought it was important to give kids a good background in grammar. I've had them learn parts of speech, diagram sentences, and do grammar exercises. Now they tell me that none of this will help them write better, that I've really been wasting my time.

Brown: Of course I don't agree with all these newfangled ideas about not teaching grammar, but if I did, I would just change. Poof, new linguistics in my classes.

Carlucci: You make it sound so easy. "Poof" and everything changes. Do you have some magic potion in your lab that will turn me into a linguist? I think it's hard to change, it's scary.

Schutz: I've never thought about it, but I suppose you're right. It is frightening to change. That book *Future Shock* talked about the impact change has on people.

Motz: Well, of course, we historians view change in larger terms; history, after all, records change.

Carlucci: Yes, change goes on all the time, but I have trouble keeping up with it. I never took a course titled "Change 101."

Schutz: That's it, we need a course in how to change. Ellen's lab doesn't have any magic potions, and anyway I think there is more to changing than going "poof."

Brown: I suppose you're right. I remember reading somewhere that change is a process.

Schutz: Well, it seems as if change is more of a process than a poof.

Burr: Ah, yes, the change process. My brother-in-law is in community development, which means he tries to help people solve community problems, and he is always talking about the change process. If the process goes on as long as he talks, it must be endless.

Schutz: I don't know very much about the change process, but I've heard . . . *(bell).*

2 Language Attitudes and the Change Process

Conflict. Arthur Koestler calls it the intersection of two disparate matrices. Thomas Kuhn calls it the awareness of anomaly. Contemporary psychologists label it psychological imbalance or dissonance. Whatever the label, conflict is familiar to us as English teachers: knowing something about alternative approaches to language, we still flinch at usages such as "between you and I," and "everyone has their pencils." Misgivings and uncertainties prompt questions: What shall we teach our students about language? Should we concern ourselves with "correctness" or "appropriateness" in language? Voices within the profession offer contradictory advice:

> endorse students' right to their own language/*insist that all students use standard English*
>
> basics are the ability to think, to use language effectively, to understand and evaluate the language of others/*basics are spelling tests, grammar drills, and weekly themes*
>
> the English language is fine and we ought to find more important things to worry about/*the English language is on its way to destruction because it is so badly used*

Change agents can use this confusion and uncertainty as a positive force. Koestler, among others, sees confrontation as the condition necessary for creative work.[1] Scientists such as Kuhn feel that recognizing deviation is the first step toward new discovery—and change.[2] But change makes people feel anxious, unnatural, even fearful. It becomes a negative force. English teachers' discomfort may stem from the suspicion that there *is* a conflict between what we know about language and what we teach in our classrooms. As students, our educational system equipped us to learn and assimilate information but not to develop new approaches. In fact, much of our education seemed calculated to insulate us from change. Textbooks usually offer a static view of the world, and few schools or teachers have kept pace with the massive social changes of the past fifty years. Teachers must remember that change is a *process* that requires creativity and a scientific approach. Our objective and subjective realities counterbalance each other. On the one hand, objective reality provides us with empirical evidence about language, allowing us to see the differences between current usage and textbook grammar. Scientific detachment enables us to look beyond the familiar and to make new discoveries. On the other hand, subjective reality dictates our affective responses to language. Our attitudes, be they conscious or subconscious, cause us to accept or reject people because of the way they speak. This constant tension can be transformed into energy, energy that can be used to spur constructive change. It is this change that clarifies our thinking and enables us to develop more continuity between what we know and what we teach.

English Teachers and Change in the Past

Changing attitudes toward language may be less intimidating if we put such change in context. William Barclay, writing twenty years ago, offers one perspective on the study of language:

> In the ancient world no one was interested in foreign languages, apart from Greek. There was no learning and no studying of foreign languages. The Greeks were the scholars, and they would never have deigned to study a barbarian tongue. The science of language is a new science, and the desire to know other languages a new desire. As Max Füller wrote: "Not till that word barbarian is struck out of the dictionary of mankind and replaced by brother, not till the right of all nations of the world to be classed as members of one genus or kind is recognized, can we look even for the first beginnings of our science of language."[3]

Although Barclay overlooks Panini and other Sanskrit scholars, whose examination of sounds and structures led to articulation of rules for Sanskrit word formation, he is generally correct. From Plato to Dionysius Thrax, Greek students of language focused on their own language; European languages were not described precisely until the late nineteenth century. Barclay's statement on the origins of linguistics reminds us of an important truth: modern linguistic study derives from an attitude change.

Linguistic study has often included attention to attitudes toward language. Robert Lowth, for example, urged attitudes of reform, purification, and standardization of language in his *Introduction to English Grammar* (1762). Lowth lamented the loss of older forms of language and saw literature rather than common speech as the source of "proper" English. Joseph Priestly, a contemporary of Lowth's, advocated a much different attitude toward language. Rather than lamenting lost forms, Priestly's *Rudiments of English Grammar* (1761) stressed that customary speech rather than past writing should constitute the standard of language. Although they differed in their views of language, both men recognized the power of attitudes toward language and pointed to attitudes which they felt needed changing. Similarly, Lowth's followers—such as Alonzo Reed and Brainerd Kellogg, authors of *Work on English Grammar and Composition* (1877), who played a major role in establishing the school tradition of language study—promoted prescriptive attitudes toward language. During the same century historical views of language generated more liberal attitudes toward usage. Works such as the several volumes of Franz Bopp's *Comparative Grammar* (1833, 1856-61, 1868-70) and Jacob Grimm's *Germanic Grammar* (1822) delineated language change, preparing the way for a school of late-nineteenth century linguists known as Neogrammarians. Centered in Leipzig, Neogrammarians viewed language change as a sign of vitality rather than decadence and urged standards based upon contemporary language rather than arbitrary rules. (Excerpts from these and other linguists are available in Diane D. Bornstein, *Readings in the Theory of Grammar from the 17th to the 20th Century* [Cambridge, Mass.: Winthrop, 1976].)

Concern with changing attitudes toward language also characterizes our more recent heritage as English teachers. Two years before the National Council of Teachers of English was organized, George Philip Krapp's *Modern English: Its Growth and Present Use* (1909) was published. Advocating social utility as the basis for linguistic standards, Krapp's views influenced many of the early leaders of NCTE. In keeping with this heritage NCTE leaders have consistently acknowledged attitude changes toward and practices of teaching language. NCTE's first monograph, Sterling Leonard's *Current English Usage* published in 1932, detailed the "questionable" usages accepted by prominent writers and editors. In 1943 *The English Journal* offered this response to a question on correct use of *don't* and *doesn't*:

> The forms *don't* and *doesn't* in the third person singular are rival forms, differing in connotation. Both are very old, both widespread among native English speakers, both immediately intelligible, both "pure" English (in sound, formation, meaning, history). There is, however, in certain groups a prejudice against *don't;* the speaker will find this a handicap to him (exactly as he will find "bad" table manners a handicap) in these groups.[4]

In 1933 Robert Pooley lamented the reactionary attitudes of textbooks toward language and urged NCTE to use every means available to make the results of research known to teachers.[5] In 1956 NCTE's Commission on the English Curriculum made this statement on usage: 1) language changes constantly; 2) change in language is normal; 3) the spoken language is primary; 4) correctness rests upon usage; 5) all usage is relative.[6] More recently Lightner investigated English teaching and found much the same situation as Pooley had twenty years earlier. In a 1965 publication Lightner wrote: "I was disconcerted to find that such a thing as formal grammar, which, as subject of much controversy, had been judged inappropriate for high school study as much as twenty years ago, is still very much a part of the curriculum. ... English teachers, it seems, could benefit from attention to their professional journals."[7]

Pooley, Lightner, and many others within the profession have thought about change, but they have viewed change narrowly, focusing on the product or desired goal and looking to professional journals as the means of reorienting English teachers. This focus on product rather than process seems to have limited the effectiveness of the effort, just as it has limited the teaching of composition. Viewing writing as process rather than product enables teachers to become more effective composition instructors. So too, thinking of change—specifically the changing of attitudes toward language—as process can produce more effective language teaching. How can teachers, then, create a process for changing attitudes toward language?

The Academic Approach to Change

One way to understand change is to look at its various forms. The one used most frequently by NCTE leaders and others prominent in the profession can be described as an academic strategy. Academic strategists assume that people are rational, that if enough facts are presented people will change. Writing articles and books is the usual deployment of this strategy, and the professional stature of the author determines the effectiveness of the effort. The theory is that if experts such as Marckwardt and Pooley offer reasons for English teachers to change the way they teach, there will undoubtedly be appropriate changes in classrooms across the country. This is simply not the case. Formal grammar continues to dominate many curricula. Detached and disinterested study, the hallmark of scholarly work, is also one of the downfalls of the academic strategy. Detachment prohibits the researcher from assuming an advocacy role. In 1956, Harold Allen, director of the Linguistic Atlas of the Upper Midwest, reported data useful to English teachers,[8] yet the academic stance of objectivity prevented him from actively rallying support.

Academic specialization offers another obstacle to change. Researchers focus on one aspect of language, become expert in it, and formulate language concepts. This research is either inaccessible to the classroom teacher, or requires more time and energy than most English teachers have. How many of our colleagues rush to read research documents issued by the Center for Applied Linguistics?

The time required to translate new information into action constitutes yet another liability of the academic strategy. Many hours are needed to construct new language units but very few to review familiar ones. Great efforts of will—the sort engendered by significant attitude change—are required for teachers to resist workbook drills on parts of speech and to devise language awareness inventories or exercises on the referential and expressive functions of language.

The most compelling drawback of the academic approach to change, however, is its lack of attention to the actual process of change. Academic strategists are idealists, concentrating on the desired end rather than on the intervening steps that lead to a goal. In fact, "strategist" may be an inaccurate term because few practitioners of the academic approach give attention to the details of practical application; few deal with how research results should be implemented. William Labov provides invaluable information about English dialects, and even delineates theoretical educational issues of the dialect controversy in his *Study of Nonstandard English,* but teachers are still left to decide for themselves how best to implement these theories.[9]

The academic strategy provides much valuable information, but we need more effective strategies to change attitudes toward language. When we ask people to change their view of language, we are asking them to do more than accept new information; we are asking them to shift their world-view. Significant relationships, values, and, of course, cherished myths come into question. People reveal strong feelings about language in conversation; sparkling eyes and looks of delight may accompany discussions of someone else's errors; a sermonic quality often characterizes proclamations on the state of the English language, whether those statements lament or approve current usage; and, as the media have proved, discussions of language attract large and responsive audiences. Part of the zealousness for particular positions may derive from the insecurity which most people feel about language. Speakers of American English are usually categorized as anxious rather than assured or indifferent, and Labov's work documents the extent of this insecurity.[10] Language myths, which are grounded in both subjective and objective reality and often appear in metaphors which control patterns of thinking and perceiving, also contribute to people's strong feelings about language. Obviously, more than a distant goal or theoretical construct is required to facilitate change in attitudes toward language. Specific methods of intervention, especially the delineation of the intervening steps between existing and desired states, are required when we approach this mixture of insecurity and myth.

Adaptive Change

Change strategists have developed a considerable body of knowledge in the past few decades; indeed, the vast and complex material on the change process poses a problem of distillation rather than development for those interested in changing attitudes toward language. (See books by Warren Bennis, Ronald Havelock, and Ronald Lippit listed in the bibliography.) Although change has always been part of the human condition, induced change is a relatively new phenomenon, and contemporary theorists are still developing and refining strategies. In this book we have attempted to distill change theory, especially attitude change, in order to extract those features most useful to teachers.

The most generally accepted theory of induced change is summarized in Kurt Lewin's three-stage model: unfreezing or developing the need for change, moving or working toward change, and freezing or stabilization.[11] Parts of this model are applicable to changing attitudes toward language, but the third stage, freezing or stabilization, implies a terminal state. It assumes that the adoption of a particular mechanism or procedure is the desired goal and signifies satisfactory completion of the change process. Adoptive change is appropriate when the goal is the diffusion of technological innovation, but it is not appropriate for refashioning myths about language. To the extent that members of our profession have considered the change process at all, however, they have tended to see it in adoptive terms.

Because knowledge about the nature of language is continually developing, it is important to maintain a flexible attitude. This calls for *adaptive* change, which stresses group participation and encourages group members to continue the change process themselves. We hope that English teachers and those they influence will become more open to change, for as Pooley puts it: "Indeed the primary force behind nearly all efforts to correct and 'purify' the English language has been the distrust of change."[12] The truth of Pooley's assertion is evident in the following statement by one such purist, Edwin Newman: "I believe that the decline in language stems in part from large causes. One of those causes is the great and rapid change this country went through in the 1960s."[13]

Changing an attitude is obviously more complicated than changing from one breakfast cereal to another or cultivating a new habit, such as fastening car seat belts. Theoretical definitions of attitude vary, but most agree that attitude consists of three dimensions: cognitive, affective, and behavioral. When attempting to change attitudes toward language, then, we must appeal to all three levels. The importance—and difficulty—of this task becomes evident as we outline the five essential steps in the change process: awareness, interest, evaluation, trial, and adoption/adaptation.

Awareness

The first and most important part of the change process is awareness of an issue. Chapter One reviewed some of the conflicting attitudes toward language; here we list eight statements which underlie an "enlightened" approach to language. These statements reflect a conscious application of knowledge about language rather than the mindless repetition of patterned responses.

1. *The English language changes continually, and if it should cease to change it will no longer be a sufficient medium for human communication.* This change is multidimensional, embracing lexical, syntactic and phonetic aspects of language. Indeed, language change has psychological dimensions. Vygotsky explains: "In the historical evolution of language the very structure of meaning and its psychological nature also change. . . . It is not merely the content of a word that changes, but the way in which reality is generalized and reflected in a word."[14] Poirier offers a contemporary illustration of the psychological aspects of language change in relating an incident involving MLA. After the chaos of the 1968 Democratic Convention in Chicago, members of the Modern Language Association were polled to decide if their own

1969 convention should be moved to another city. Arguments for and against such a move were presented. Critics of the ballot suggested that it stressed the complication of rearranging hotel accommodations, biasing the reader in favor of keeping the convention in Chicago.

> The framers of the MLA ballot designed to poll the members about a 1969 meeting in Chicago did not recognize the changed context for words that a few months earlier would have been neutral enough. They were appalled at the evidence that their language expressed intentions they hadn't at all meant to express. How did it happen that their wording confused hotel space with political space and implied a primary concern with the former? The critics of the ballot were astonished, perhaps in my own case too self-righteously so, that anyone committed to the study of language could think it possible, in the fall of 1968, to say or write anything, especially on such a subject as Chicago, which would not invite political readings.
> That's a small example of what's meant by saying that no one speaks as he once did and means what he once did: the word Chicago had been made a political word. It was no longer simply a geographical one. And it had been changed, that word, not by an Academy, but by the Mayor of Chicago.[15]

2. *Language change does not equal language decay.* Change is one indication of vitality, a natural and necessary expression of life. Who would argue that Chaucer's "Whan that Aprille with his shoures sote" was more effective communication for the people of his time than Adrienne Rich's line, "When they mow the fields, I see the world reformed as if by snow, or fire or physical desire" is today? Carried to its logical extreme, the "change equals decay" argument assumes that effective communication will soon cease. Indeed, Jean Stafford predicts the demise of the language: "Besides the neologisms that are splashed all over the body of the American language like the daubings of a chimpanzee turned loose with finger paints, the poor thing has had its parts of speech broken to smithereens. . . . The prognosis for the ailing language is not good. I predict that it will not die in my lifetime, but I fear that it will be assailed by countless cerebral accidents and massive strokes and gross insults to the brain and finally will no longer be able to sit up in bed and take nourishment by mouth."[16] Stafford might well consider the words of Vygotsky: "A spontaneous utterance, wrong from the point of view of grammar, may have charm and aesthetic value. Absolute correctness is achieved only beyond natural language, in mathematics"[17] or Britton: "The real pedant sees change in everything that leads to the language as he learnt it, but regards all subsequent changes as decay."[18] Hall goes

so far as to argue that the human nervous system has limited capacity for rigorous adherence to fixed norms of behavior and asserts that "for the past million years, the human race has changed linguistically *instead* of biologically—culture and its changes, rather than biological change, are our mechanism of adaptation to environment."[19]

3. *Attitudes are central to language.* Registers of speech—the difference between recounting an accident to a sympathetic spouse and to a judge and jury—are but one reflection of the complex intermingling of attitudes and language. Attitudes about self and audience determine many of the lexical, phonetic, and syntactic choices made by a speaker or writer. Labov's study of linguistic change on Martha's Vineyard demonstrates the influence of self-perception upon linguistic features. Centralization of diphthongs /ay/ and /aw/ in words such as *right, ride, my, about,* and *down* was obvious in "those who laid claim to native status as Vineyarders . . . while those who were excluded from this status or who abandoned their claims to pursue a career on the mainland, would show no centralization of these vowels."[20] At the same time attitudes toward others are shaped by language. As Fraser puts it, "There is general agreement that the way a person speaks is often coupled—frequently with little or no justification—with a stereotypic level of education, social status, degree of friendliness, and so forth."[21] Attitudes, then, play a major role in both production and reception of speech.

4. *Current attitudes about language and language instruction cover a wide spectrum of opinion.* Two statements represent this range: "Textbooks used in the study of the English language must teach that traditional rules of grammar are a worthwhile subject for academic pursuit and are essential for effective communication."[22] "And intelligibility itself is not only a complex function of features of linguistic form (phonological, lexical, syntactic), but also of norms of interaction and conduct in conversation, and of attitudes toward differences in all these respects."[23] The first statement reflects a functional attitude toward language; correct language serves as a means for effective communication. It assumes that correctness is essential to communication and implies an authoritarian approach to language instruction. The second statement emphasizes the political aspects of language— sorting and limiting lives, restricting entry into privileged groups. It assumes that styles of communication serve as social markers. The descriptive perspective here suggests a scientific rather than an authoritarian view of language.

5. *English teachers transmit attitudes toward language.* We are all painfully familiar with the typical response to the introduction of an English teacher, "Oh, I'd better watch my grammar." Yet that response has been earned by many English teachers who have emphasized certain forms of language and punished students who used others. Vonnegut describes the linguistic insecurity engendered by English teachers: "Most white people in Midland City were insecure when they spoke, so they kept their sentences short and their words simple, in order to keep embarrassing mistakes to a minimum. . . . This was because their English teachers would wince and cover their ears and give them flunking grades and so on whenever they failed to speak like English aristocrats before the First World War."[24] Whether they view themselves as upholders of sacred tradition or as liberators of linguistically based discrimination patterns, English teachers have impact upon society's attitudes toward language. Their continuing presence on usage panels for dictionaries is but one example of their suasive power.

6. *Public opinion and attitude lag behind usage patterns.* As in other fields of human behavior, hypocrisy or inconsistency often intervene between proclamation and practice. Labov's New York City study provides an index of the differences between what people say and what they think they should say.[25] Standard English, then, contains a much wider array of usages than the general public's statements about language would indicate.

7. *Teacher attitudes toward language have implications for all aspects of teaching.* Empirical evidence indicates that average citizens make stereotypic assumptions based on speech patterns, and English teachers are not exempt from unexamined views. Indeed, "A study of teachers' attitudes in primary school has shown that the child's ability to use the linguistic table-manners his teacher expects is a key element in determining not only the teacher's attitude to the child, but his assessment of his potential as a learner."[26] Research has demonstrated the power of self-fulfilling prophecy or the Pygmalion phenomenon in education.[27]

8. *English teachers receive as well as transmit attitudes toward language.* Students, of course, are their most immediate audience, but students also bring to the classroom a variety of usage patterns and attitudes toward language. The English teacher's response—whether acceptance, correction, or hostility—to these attitudes and usages is an important part of the classroom setting. In addition, students, especially young children, bring their developmental

processes to the classroom; the close correlation between language growth and other forms of development has many implications. For example, as Piaget's work has shown, all children go through an absolutist stage in their attitude toward rules and insist upon "correct" answers for language along with everything else.[28] According to Hotopf, English teachers cannot be held responsible for normative attitudes toward language: "Even if teachers taught differently, we should probably still have the ontogenetic recapitulation of the 18th century's attitude to language in everybody's life history."[29]

Colleagues within any educational system exert another sort of pressure upon English teachers. All but the most enlightened teachers in other disciplines assume that writing and general language training are solely the responsibility of the English teacher. Products of prescriptive approaches to grammar, many teachers of subjects other than English retain the attendant language myths and hold the English teacher responsible for enforcing an absolute standard. English teachers are faced with educating colleagues as well as students, showing that language instruction is the responsibility of all who teach, and making colleagues aware of alternatives to prescriptive approaches.

The general public also has unsuitable expectations of English teachers, and the media often reinforce these expectations. Users of Ultra Brite toothpaste, who spell "brite" for "bright"; low scorers on verbal sections of standardized tests; applicants unable to fill out forms—these people exemplify a small number of the "sins" for which English teachers are held responsible. The now legendary issue of *Newsweek* (December 5, 1975) that focused on student writing ability generated a succession of articles lamenting the inadequacies of English teachers. Teachers outside the discipline of English and much of the general public are convinced that there are "right" answers to all questions of usage and that English teachers are responsible for ensuring that students master the correct forms. These people do not seem to recognize the teaching of effective or interesting expression as an important goal of English curriculum.

These eight statements suggest the breadth of awareness necessary for anyone considering changing attitudes toward language. At the same time, the complexity of each item suggests that more than cognitive awareness is involved. Awareness, like attitudes, includes dimensions of knowing, feeling, and behaving.

Interest

Being aware of NCTE's statement on students' right to their own language is still a far cry from implementing that statement in class. Just as motivation is both the most important and the most elusive factor in education, so is interest in change both crucial and difficult to instill. Efforts to motivate students have had limited success, and strategies for producing a desire to change are likewise tenuous. However, teachers have continued to find ways to interest students in learning, and we have found it possible to engage people in changing attitudes toward language.

Both internal and external forces provide impetus to change. Two powerful examples that affect most English teachers are dissatisfaction with the present system and outside pressure. One glance at current professional journals reveals one source of dissatisfaction—an abundance of articles testifying to the impossible tasks facing English teachers, and the lack of community support for their work. We believe this view is held by a majority of competent professionals who are receiving no positive reinforcement and are frequently confronted by claims from within and outside the profession that their teaching is misguided and/or is not producing desired results. Some teachers reject sources that question their competence, but guilt and anxiety, common reactions to lack of reinforcement, plague others. This sense of inadequacy and the fear that they are failing to live up to the expectations of valued associates may actually condition some English teachers to be open to change.

Outside pressure not only contributes to guilt and anxiety but also operates forcefully on its own terms. Parents suing a school system because a graduating child is functionally illiterate create tremendous external pressure for change. Similarly, public demands for "literacy," for the economy of larger classes, for the reassurance of standardized tests, coupled with media attention (largely negative) to the activities of the English class, exert enormous pressure for change. But outside pressures can also work in positive ways. A curriculum coordinator who shelves an existing language program and invites teachers to construct a new one represents an external force that opens the way for change.

Evaluation

Ready for change, English teachers, or any other group, search for and evaluate alternatives. Written material provides one source of new approaches, but that alone is not strong enough to effect change. The most effective means of ensuring thoughtful evaluation of new ideas and practices is through a change agent, someone who can link needs with available resources. One function served by change agents is to offer demonstrations of new approaches to language. For instance, a linguistically based diagnostic approach to spelling can be demonstrated by categorizing and defining spelling errors on an actual student paper. This captures the interest of teachers frustrated with filling margins with "sp," and gives them an opportunity to evaluate the merits of a new view of language. Change agents can also emphasize the practical benefits of a linguistic approach that reduces the time required to grade papers while it improves student writing. Of course, the reduction of guilt and anxiety is a compelling practical benefit and plays an important role in the evaluation process.

Inevitably, evaluation involves a recapitulation of the awareness step in the change process, but this time each factor is carefully scrutinized; we read more thoroughly that which affects us directly. There are two methods for acquiring information on new approaches: identification and scanning.

Identification usually focuses on the change agent and can produce positive or negative reactions. *Negative identification* generally occurs when change agents emphasize their official role, when a group is captive and cannot avoid participation, when a group feels helpless or threatened, or when change is mandated. Response to negative identification is typically narrow and stilted, often resulting in rote implementation of suggested approaches. When a department chair, for example, insists that all department members participate in an inservice program and submit documentation of their use of the new approach to language, teachers will tend to transport ideas directly into their classes without considering variations among teaching situations. University "experts" who appear for one-day presentations in secondary or elementary schools are also likely to inspire negative identification.

Positive identification, on the other hand, occurs when the target group is voluntary, can leave at any time, trusts the change agent, and faces no enforcement of change. In this situation, change agents do not emphasize formal positions and allow the target group considerable autonomy. Change resulting from positive identification is generally spontaneous, enlarging, differentiated and supportive of further growth.

Scanning, in contrast to identification, is an information-gathering process. In this case a change agent serves as a resource person, making information available to group members. Although a group can initiate its own survey, a knowledgeable change agent can certainly facilitate the process. Scanning the positions advocated by Edwin Newman, Harold Allen, and William Labov, for example, could give teachers a clear idea of the range of attitudes toward language and enable them to formulate their own positions more accurately. Similarly, a group wishing to explore new teaching strategies might add to written resources by soliciting successful approaches from colleagues.

Trial

The evaluation stage, if successful, leads to *intention.* Having become aware of a problem, developed an interest in it, and evaluated various approaches, a group needs direct experience with new methods. Educational theory admonishes us to rely on experiential learning in class, but teachers often neglect this dimension in their own learning. How many times have we taken a course in the teaching of composition and not done any writing ourselves? What about language courses that discuss regional dialects but never ask students to survey speakers in their own neighborhoods? Testing new skills is particularly important in the change process because without such testing people are very likely to return to habitual routines and forget new ideas. The task of changing attitudes toward language requires attention to behavior and feelings as well as to intellectual comprehension. Thus trial is crucial in the change process. English teachers who are considering a descriptive rather than a prescriptive approach to grammar should have opportunities to "try out" new approaches. Responding to a student's "I ain't got no pencil" in hypothetical situations, evaluating student papers within the group, simulating the giving of instructions to students embarking upon field study, doing field study oneself, or teaching a mini-lesson on usage patterns are a few examples of the kinds of experimentation that can prepare English teachers to continue the change process.

Adoption/Adaptation

The ultimate success of the change process rests in adoption/adaptation. The change process is no more effective than authoritarian exhortation if it does not lead to the inclination for altering ideas and approaches. Changes in attitudes toward language manifest themselves in new feelings and changed behaviors in and outside the classroom. When we recall the enormous energy required to make a very simple change in behavior—the exhaustion which accompanies the beginning of a new term as we adapt to different schedules and new rooms, for example—we see the importance of adoption/adaptation in the change process.

It is at the adoption/adaptation stage that support for change becomes essential. Teachers can be aware of and interested in new approaches. They can evaluate alternatives and even subject some to trial, but maintaining a positive disposition toward change and adopting novel practices in the classroom assume support from peers and superiors. It can be futile, even dangerous, to take a flexible approach to language when one teaches in a school where an authoritarian view of language prevails. Even if passive acceptance or active interest in new views exists, change is not guaranteed. First attempts are fraught with difficulties, and a support group is often necessary to prevent an innovator from abandoning the new in favor of the familiar. A support group can be as informal as two other teachers who are trying similar things and are willing to discuss their successes and failures, or as formal as a class where evaluations occur systematically.

As we said earlier, adaptive rather than adoptive change is the goal. Adaptation as applied to language attitudes does not imply initiating a particular program of study or buying a specific text—although these and other adoptions might be part of the process. Rather, we urge teachers to cultivate an increased willingness to change. Just as change in language implies vitality, so an equally vital response is necessary to keep pace with changes in our understanding of language. The nature of language and our growing understanding of it demand that we adapt our perspectives rather than insist upon adopting a single stance. Adoption of an adaptive attitude toward language is, finally, the goal.

Facilitating Change in Language Attitudes

Although the stages of the change process from awareness to adoption/adaptation follow one another logically, they do not occur without conscious effort. Those who can encourage and guide this effort are called change agents. A change agent must be acquainted with the change process, aware of available resources (though not necessarily familiar with all of them), and able to help a group to define and reach its goals. But this designation need not be formal; agents' official positions vary from curriculum coordinator to college/university faculty member, to secondary school faculty member, to interested citizen.

Whatever their position, change agents need to *know the local environment.* If, for example, a group has had little exposure to contemporary linguistic study and believes in the merits of traditional grammar, it will be less receptive to changing attitudes than a group familiar with current linguistic work. Change agents who know their audience will be able to predict reactions before new ideas and schemes are introduced and thus avoid alienating participants. Of course, the social structure of the target group is an integral part of the local environment. Change agents working in an English department, for example, need to know which individuals have power within the group and how they use that power. A very effective program for initiating attitude changes can be useless if the department is dominated by an unreceptive chair who intimidates other department members. Knowing the local environment also enables change agents to build upon existing patterns and attitudes; new ways can be grafted onto old. Timing, a crucial element in any change process, can be vastly improved if agents know the target group well. Needs of which the group is aware serve as an excellent starting point for change, and change agents are always more effective when they know the expectations the group brings to the change process. Change agents also need to understand outside pressures upon and dissatisfactions within the group.

Involving group members is essential since investment derives from involvement. In addition to providing further information about the local environment, involving the target group accomplishes valuable linguistic tasks. One of the most pressing needs in contemporary linguistics is to study existing usage patterns. Labov and others have demonstrated the value of determining how people actually express themselves rather than surveying how they think they should talk. Group members can conduct studies of usage patterns, thereby increasing their active involvement and gaining first-hand knowledge of usage variation.

One of the real challenges for any change agent is to *maintain a distinction between role and person.* We've all known lawyers who can't refrain from treating guests like clients, ministers who preach at everyone they meet, even teachers who instruct everyone within earshot—people so immersed in their professional roles that they have forgotten how to function as persons. It is tempting for the change agent to fall into the same trap. Take a little expertise, add a little responsibility for others, and it is easy to produce a change agent who takes refuge in playing a role. Yet the personal characteristics of the change agent determine much of the success or failure in innovation. The change agent who has the greatest success responds to group needs rather than imposing an agenda upon the group, emphasizes personal qualities rather than formal credentials, doesn't insist upon adoption of a particular idea but helps the group become comfortable with alternatives to present practice. Ideally change agents, aside from their knowledgeability about language, should be more than amiable persons who merely convene a group of teachers for a discussion of language. Knowing how deeply held attitudes toward language typically are, the most effective agent will be one who carefully and sensitively introduces new ideas. And, finally, it is the person, not the role of change agent, that enables a group to develop sufficient self-awareness to consider the implications of its own attitudes toward language.

One final but extremely important qualification for change agents is the ability to use a variety of intervention strategies. These strategies, defined below, help the agent cope with attitudes and behaviors likely to be found in a group situation, and help ensure that the group is productive.

Discrepancy intervention calls attention to the contradictions and discrepancies in an existing situation. It takes little imagination to think of discrepancies between current linguistic knowledge and dominant practices of language teaching, and the ongoing work of linguistic researchers continues to expose others. Similarly, even the most prescriptive English teachers must be aware of the contradictions between grammar book pronouncements and the language of educated and accomplished people. More sophisticated English teachers notice the contradiction between the prevailing American myth of linguistic uniformity and the substantial variety in American speech. Discrepancy intervention frequently draws upon or accompanies *theory intervention* which, through research and theoretical implications, provides empirical or rhetorical constructs for noting discrepancies in current practices. For our purposes, these two forms of intervention may be considered a single form.

Discrepancy intervention can be used by academics and others well removed from school language classes; however, *procedural intervention* requires more direct contact between change agent and group participants and is therefore more productive. This form of intervention examines existing programs to determine if more effective procedures can be employed. Secondary and primary English teachers with some linguistic background and willingness to search out resources can use procedural intervention effectively.

Relationship intervention is often necessary as a group becomes involved in the change process and tensions develop between members who hold different views about language. Any suggestion of change arouses a certain amount of hostility and anxiety, but discussions of changing attitudes toward language often produce great tensions. Courtney Cazden's investigation of the attitudes of black parents in Boston toward language and language education reveals the powerful emotions generated by discussions of language.[30] A change agent who uses relationship intervention cannot rely upon an authoritarian role but must be responsive to a variety of viewpoints.

Later in the change process, after awareness and interest are evident, *dilemma intervention* may occur. This involves examining assumptions about language and identifying the significant alternatives in language instruction, searching for those that fall between the extreme positions of theory and practice. Dilemma intervention requires a wide-ranging view of linguistic issues, one which is difficult to extrapolate from many of the single-issue approaches offered in linguistic research. The change agent must coordinate such disparate factors as research in teacher attitudes toward various dialects, sentence combining as an alternative to traditional grammar, and prohibitions against fitting students to the language curriculum.

Organization structure intervention involves identifying issues of language controversy that derive from the educational or social structures to which group members belong. A school may, for example, require tests that measure a narrow spectrum of linguistic usages. Organizational intervention is very effective when desired change affects only one structure—decreasing factory workers' dissatisfaction, for example—but attitudes toward language extend beyond any one structure and into society as a whole. The complex relationship between society and language makes structural intervention difficult, but sociolinguistic studies such as William Labov's examination of relationships between language and social status (cited in note 5 of Chapter One and note 20 of Chapter Two) suggest models for organization.

Perspective intervention provides historical understanding of the language controversy, and can create healthy distance when emotions about language run high. Thomas Lounsbury's book, *The Standard of English Usage,* argues that speakers of a language must be dead—intellectually if not physically—before that language will become fixed.[31] Tracing usage controversies from the seventeenth century forward and citing influential authors from many periods, Lounsbury illustrates the shifts in what is defined as good English. Lounsbury's book offers a sweeping perspective on usage controversies, and its publication seventy years ago demonstrates that today's disputes are not unique. A more contemporary text, Arthur Applebee's *Tradition and Reform in the Teaching of English: A History,* discusses the changing attitudes of English teachers toward language.[32] A change agent can draw upon these and more general publications to remind a group that many of today's problems and controversies are not new. The professional memory is surprisingly short and, as long-time readers of professional journals can attest, the same ideas have a way of reappearing every few years. Perspective intervention can encourage a historical view of language instruction.

Discussions about changing attitudes toward language are, in the final analysis, circular. What we, as humans, know and believe—our attitudes toward language—are based in language itself. We are verbal creatures, and our language about language determines many of our attitudes toward language; yet changing our language about language requires a change in attitude toward language. The problem we face is reflexive: its subject and object are identical. Yet, as this chapter has illustrated, the change process—not instant change—has potential for changing attitudes toward language. In this chapter, we have tried to establish a theoretical basis for linking the change process with attitudes toward language; now we shall illustrate practical applications of this theoretical construct.

Notes

1. Arthur Koestler, *The Act of Creation* (New York: The Macmillan Company, 1964), p. 96.

2. Thomas Kuhn, *The Structure of Scientific Revolutions* (Chicago: University of Chicago Press, 1962), p. 52.

3. William Barclay, *The Letters to the Phillippians, Colossians and Thessalonians* (Philadelphia: Westminster Press, 1959), p. 186.

4. P. G. Perrin, Albert H. Marckwardt and J. B. McMillan, "Current English Forum," *English Journal* 32 (November 1943): 519-20.

5. Robert C. Pooley, "Grammar and Usage in Composition Textbooks," *English Journal* 22 (January 1933): 18.

6. Charles V. Hartung, "Doctrines of English Usage," *English Journal* 45 (December 1956): 517.

7. C. Michael Lightner, "1930-1945," in *An Examination of the Attitudes of the NCTE Toward Language*, ed. Raven I. McDavid, Jr. (Urbana, Ill.: NCTE, 1965), p. 29.

8. Harold Allen, "The Linguistic Atlases: Our New Resource," *English Journal* 45 (April 1956): 188-94.

9. William Labov, *The Study of Nonstandard English* (Urbana, Ill.: NCTE, 1970).

10. William D. Labov, *The Social Stratification of English in New York* (Washington, D.C.: Center for Applied Linguistics, 1966).

11. Kurt Lewin, "Frontiers in Group Dynamics: Concept, Method and Reality in Social Science," *Human Relations* 1 (1947): 5-42.

12. Robert C. Pooley, *The Teaching of English Usage*, p. 25.

13. Edwin Newman, *Strictly Speaking* (Indianapolis: Bobbs-Merrill, 1974), p. 9.

14. L. S. Vygotsky, *Thought and Language* (Cambridge, Mass.: MIT Press, 1962), pp. 212-13.

15. Richard Poirier, "What Is English Studies, and If You Know What That Is, What Is English Literature?" *Partisan Review* 37, no. 1 (1970): 47.

16. Jean Stafford, "Plight of the American Language," *Saturday Review/World*, 4 December 1973, p. 14.

17. Vygotsky, *Thought and Language*, p. 127.

18. James Britton, *Language and Learning* (Middlesex, England: Penguin Books, 1970), p. 134.

19. Robert A. Hall, Jr., *Leave Your Language Alone* (Ithaca, N.Y.: Linguistica, 1950), pp. 183-84.

20. William D. Labov, "The Effect of Social Mobility on Linguistic Behavior," *Sociological Inquiry* 36 (1966): 187.

21. Bruce Fraser, "Some 'Unexpected' Reactions to Various American-English Dialects," in *Language Attitudes*, ed. Roger W. Shuy and Ralph W. Fasold, p. 28.

22. *Charleston Gazette*, 22 November 1974, 1A and 8A, as quoted in Allan A. Glatthorn, "Censorship and the Classroom Teacher," *English Journal* 66 (February 1977): 14.

23. Dell Hymes, "Speech and Language: On the Origins and Foundations of Inequality Among Speakers," *Daedalus* 102 (Summer 1973): 65.

24. Kurt Vonnegut, Jr., *Breakfast of Champions* (New York: Dell, 1974), p. 142.

25. Labov, *Social Stratification*.

26. Anthony Adams, *Team-Teaching and the Teaching of English* (Oxford: Pergamon Press, 1970), p. 14.

27. R. Rosenthal and Lenore Jacobson, *Pygmalion in the Classroom* (New York: Holt, Rinehart & Winston, 1968).

28. Jean Piaget, *The Moral Judgment of the Child* (Glencoe, Ill.: The Free Press, 1948), pp. 1-103.

29. W. H. N. Hotopf, *Language, Thought and Comprehension* (Bloomington: Indiana University Press, 1965), p. 255.

30. C. Cazden, B. Bryant, and M. A. Tillman, "Making It and Going Home: The Attitudes of Black People Toward Language Education," *Harvard Graduate School of Education Association Bulletin* 14 (Spring 1970): 4-9.

31. Thomas R. Lounsbury, *The Standard of Usage in English* (New York: Harper & Brothers Publishers, 1908).

32. Arthur Applebee, *Tradition and Reform in the Teaching of English: A History* (Urbana, Ill.: NCTE, 1974).

Scene: Same place, same group, different day

Schutz *(bounding into room where others are already relaxing):* It worked! It worked! I tried it and it worked!

Motz: What worked? The coffee machine?

Schutz: No, no, my language lesson. I tried something new and it worked.

Carlucci: That's exciting! Most of the new things I try fall flat. Tell me about it.

Schutz: Well, I began the class by talking about symbols. I pointed to the flag and asked the kids what it meant. We talked about other concrete symbols like signs, wedding rings, and gestures; the kids were really sensitive to the importance of context. They seemed to get the idea that a physical symbol means approximately the same thing to all of us but that each of us has at least slightly different associations with the symbol.

Burr: A heavy idea. I've gotten at it through indexing. I remembered reading some stuff by semanticists like Hayakawa and Johnson. They suggested that we can avoid over-generalizing and stereotyping by remembering that policeman$_1$ is not policeman$_2$. The kids really dug that. For a while they were numbering just about everything they talked about.

Schutz: Right. But that wasn't quite what I wanted to get across today. I was more interested in trying out a few ideas about dialect. I'd come across a position statement from NCTE called "Students' Right to Their Own Language," and one sentence really caught my eye. I've just about memorized it: "The claim that any one dialect is unacceptable amounts to an attempt of one social group to exert its dominance over another."

Burr: Yeah. That *is* heavier than indexing.

Schutz: So, I gave them some sets of sentences at different levels of acceptability. For example, one set was "He ain't got no brains," "He isn't very smart," "He lacks intelligence." They could recognize that each sentence means almost the same thing but that deciding which to use depends on context. Each one is a dialect form, and one is not more absolutely correct than the other two. The kids seemed to understand that and talked about it so easily that I almost thought I wasn't teaching them anything new.

Carlucci: Well, it was new to hear an *English* teacher say that, I can tell you.

Schutz: Yes, I suppose you're right, and until the last few months I don't think I would have dared admit to this way of explaining correct language. *(bell)*

Motz: Sic transit gloria mundi, if I may say so. And furthermore, caveat emptor.

3 Changing Language Attitudes within the Profession

As Francis Bacon predicted in 1605, we have become a society where, in matters of learning, things "may be done by some persons, though not by everyone."[1] That is, we have become a society of professionals. As English teachers we operate within the boundaries of our profession, and our peers in other disciplines are likewise circumscribed. We may talk with the person who teaches chemistry or mathematics, but our real conversations, our explorations of significant issues, occur within our own profession. We measure our teaching successes and failures against norms created by other English teachers, not by history teachers, and we look to others within our own profession for information that shapes our approach to English studies.

Yet, we all know that within our profession there are few points of consensus. Although English teachers can count on their profession for a sense of identity which sets them apart from teachers in other disciplines, for some rewards and punishments, and for limited kinds of support in controversies such as censorship, our profession does not offer an authoritative voice on the language issue. No member of NCTE or any other professional organization determines what we as English teachers should do or believe about teaching the English language. Much as we might wish it, no exalted figure is likely to lean down and say, "Here are the answers; all the controversies have ended. Simply take this box to your classroom, and all your problems with language teaching will be solved."

Instead, we are left to muck about in the half-light of our own wisdom, searching for our own answers and methods. Yet, precisely because we are professionals, we have resources that are not available to the general public. We can accomplish things that "may be done by some persons, though not by everyone." We can call upon our training in English language and literature and upon available research, and, if we so choose, we can take an active role in exploring language issues with our colleagues. Attitudes toward language will be as adaptive as the members of our profession choose to make them.

Forming a Group

The easiest way to ensure large-scale participation in the change process is for a group or individual with authority to require teacher cooperation, either directly or indirectly. For example, a school district may sponsor an inservice program or course and require (or at least encourage) teachers to attend; an administrative mandate such as a directive from a department chair may bring department members together; or an "expert" from another school may request participation in a special project. Carrots such as free tuition or merit increases and sticks such as peer ostracism or threats from superiors often play a role in bringing such groups together. At first glance, this seems an ideal way to convene a group. People who might be intimidated by or uninterested in the topic will participate; a change agent need not waste time and energy trying to find willing participants; and many of the logistical details will be simplified. Certainly many classes fit this description, and they are not necessarily all bad. However, our experience as change agents is that a group created this way effects much less change than one formed as the result of internal need.

The difference between self-convened and externally convened groups seems to be the degree of awareness and investment. As explained in Chapter Two, awareness of an issue is the first essential stage in the change process, and externally convened groups rarely have that quality. The glazed eyes and sign-in-and-leave behavior we've observed in externally convened groups convince us that even the most modest goals may be impossible to attain in such a setting. However, we've sometimes been surprised. A polite and perfunctory department has nodded through our one-day workshop and then, we are told later, made significant revisions in its language curriculum. More often one or two members of a class or an inservice group will pursue the topic of changing attitudes toward language or start to look for other like-minded souls.

One group we know formed around a single member of an English department—not the chair—who seemed to be generally trusted and liked. The instigator had taken a course that raised linguistic questions for her. She began talking with her peers about language teaching and quickly discovered that a number of people in the department shared her concerns. She proposed that they begin meeting as a group, and the change process was begun. Other successful change groups we've known have evolved from professional associations or from groups with designated tasks such as curriculum design. Often these groups have included people from several school systems.

If you find no one in your department who cares about attitudes toward language, don't despair; there may be several interested people in the next district. Finding allies in neighboring districts can be an overt or covert process, depending upon what suits you. Advertisements in the NCTE affiliate newsletter, an open letter to all members of nearby English departments, or flyers distributed at an area inservice program are among the more explicit methods of locating interested colleagues. The Conference on Language Attitudes and Composition (CLAC) announcements which have appeared in national journals offer an example of the types of issues that can be raised:

1. If you're worried about the shoddy linguistics used to construct competency-based entry/exit tests for colleges (Georgia Regents' Exam) or
2. puzzled over the confused, hostile reaction to the CCCC "Students' Right to Their Own Language" position paper, a reaction that perceives the NCTE as monolithic or anarchistic, or
3. wrestling with problems associated with language and the teaching of composition, or
4. aware of any public policy and language planning which seems suspect, write for the CLAC Newsletter, c/o Jim Nattinger, Shelley Reece or Tony Wolk, Department of English, Portland State University, P.O. Box 751, Portland, OR 92707. We hope to be more on the side of action than suffering.

The number and quality of responses to the CLAC advertisements confirm the efficacy of overt methods. Of course individual personality, school politics, and other variables may dictate more subtle means. Our own pattern has been to inquire informally about potential participants and then invite each one personally. We've found that a group whose members represent several teaching situations is often more effective than a group from a single department. Teachers seem more comfortable raising sensitive language issues with people they won't see in the hall the next day.

If a group has no designated time limit for its existence—and few self-convened groups do—one of your first tasks is to raise the question of the group's duration. We have found that it is preferable for a group to err on the short side—better to agree to meet for one term and then renegotiate for a second term than to set a longer commitment. Guilt and other negative feelings are almost inevitable if a group sets no time limit; some members drift away feeling they haven't accomplished anything, and the remaining members harbor bitterness or a sense of failure because the group didn't stay together. We say "almost inevitable" because we know of one group where the reverse occurred. The group was composed of several concerned teachers within a system who had agreed to meet bimonthly to share a meal and concerns about language teaching. Initially, the discussions were lively, resource people were brought in frequently, and the group was optimistic about changing attitudes within the whole school. However, as time went on, group members became attached to one another, didn't want to deal with controversial issues which might offend someone, and began to pay more attention to the menus. As far as we know, this group is still sharing gourmet delights, but it has abandoned any thought of changing attitudes toward language.

If a group is self-convened, the variables of size and membership will also need to be established. We have no magic numbers to offer, but our experience suggests that a group with fewer than 10 members is too small and one with more than 20 is too large. We have found it effective to divide larger groups into smaller groups to allow individual participation and the intimacy necessary for exploring attitudes. Interest in and commitment to the group should, of course, be the chief criterion for membership. If you are in the position to choose some members and exclude others, we advise selecting teachers with three to five years of experience. Teachers with a great deal of experience tend to have firmly entrenched attitudes, and beginners are usually too insecure and uncertain to consider new ideas. Our hunches on this were validated by Taylor's study of teacher attitudes toward black and nonstandard English.[2]

Assessing Environment

Whether dealing with an externally or self-convened group, a change agent needs to become familiar with the school environment. If you are working with colleagues within a single school, this may seem a simple task, but initiating the change process requires the reassessment of familiar situations. The obvious markers of location—urban, suburban, rural—and socioeconomic level of the community determine many of the differences between schools and contribute to variables such as degree of community support and administrative structure. These forces take on increased importance when the change agent considers changing attitudes toward language. Cazden's report on the opposition of Roxbury parents to using anything but standard English to teach their preschool children suggests that the disparate forces operating in and around a school—forces which are related to vocational aspirations, social standing, and scholastic ambition—become crucial.[3]

Although each school is unique, there are also similarities that transcend place and class. Schools throughout the country face the national disillusionment with education as a panacea; whether this attitude is a legacy of the sixties or a consequence of continuing fiscal crises, citizens are generally unwilling to invest more money in schools. Tight budgets impose various forms of retrenchment, and conservative attitudes toward language (with concomitant policies and materials) are just one manifestation of the public schools' difficulties. An accompanying and perhaps related national phenomenon is increased public support for standardized tests as a means of determining college entry. According to a 1976 Gallup poll of public attitudes toward education, "A consensus was found in favor of requiring high school students to pass a standardized exam in order to receive a diploma."[4] And 84 percent of the sample felt that standardized tests are reliable. The same high percentage may not endorse the linguistic values inherent in standardized tests, but, endorsed or not, these values receive implicit support as standardized tests become more popular. Tests have a way of determining language curricula—even attitudes toward such curricula—and the narrow view of language embodied in standardized tests suggests that the nation's schools face pressures to become more single-minded and less open to changing attitudes toward language.

Another similarity among schools is the discrepancy between people of authority and people with power. If authority is defined as holding a publicly recognized position which includes directive and enforcing functions, and power is the ability to accomplish things whether through publicly recognized means or not, it is obvious that those with authority in schools may not be those with power. Influential figures often advise department chairs and other school officials; policy pronouncements that appear to come from one source may actually be dictated by another.

Approaches for eliciting affirmative responses from these two groups differ. The official sanction of the administration is nearly always necessary for any school committee and is normally readily obtainable, especially if the committee is intent on clarifying its own attitudes toward language rather than directly changing the curriculum. A careful explanation to administrators can eliminate many logistical problems as well as give credibility to the committee's work. Influential English teachers may be more difficult to deal with because their power is often covert and they may have proprietary feelings about an English department's program. The change agent must find ways to enlist their support, usually by including them in the group, giving them responsibility, and making them feel part of the change process. Those involved in decision making and change are less likely to find fault with the results.

Two of the most effective strategies for creating positive attitudes toward change—the trouble and jealousy methods—are often inherent in the school and community environments. The media have already done much to foster the trouble method. Reports of barely literate students, declining scores on standardized tests, and implicit and explicit questions about the teaching of English serve to heighten the insecurity of nearly all English teachers. The process begins: "If these things are true, we must be in trouble, and if we're in trouble we'd better do something." Administrators, and even influential English teachers within the department, may be convinced that the current "trouble" warrants consideration of change or at least a closer look at the status quo. The jealousy method also plays upon the inherent competitiveness of our society and lures people toward change associated with higher status, improved benefits, or other symbols of hierarchical relationships. For example, "X school district has just redesigned its language program. If X is doing it, then it must be good," or "Look at all the federal money Y school is getting for its new language program. Why don't we try to get a piece of the action?" Of course jealousy and trouble are not the only ways to create positive attitudes toward change. Curiosity about language, pride in one's work, an interest in furthering knowledge are also strong activating forces that should not be overlooked by the change agent.

Determining the Level of Awareness

Once a group is convened—whether for a one-day meeting required by the department, an open-ended discussion, or a college course—the change agent (teacher, visiting expert, self-appointed convener) needs to determine the level of individual and group awareness on language issues. General discussion of issues is one way of determining awareness. After necessary introductions and the formulation of group expectations, the discussion might continue something like this:

> Change Agent: We're all here because we're concerned about the teaching of language. I thought we might begin by focusing on a few questions about language to determine some of the assumptions we bring to this group. For example, how do you react to the statement, "One should always avoid contractions in written English"?
>
> Speaker 1: That's one of the things I remember being told by my own high school teacher, and I do try to avoid contractions in my own writing. But I've never really thought about it. What's wrong with contractions anyway?
>
> S2: Doesn't it have something to do with the fact that they are a sign of informality? I guess written language is supposed to be more formal than spoken language.
>
> S3: But is it always supposed to be so very formal? I can think of times—when I write my son for example—when I don't want to be so formal.
>
> S4: Yes, and what about the fact that my current issue of *The New Yorker* is full of contractions? I thought that was supposed to be a pretty highbrow magazine. If it uses contractions so freely, I'm going to have trouble telling my students that they shouldn't.
>
> S5: Well, it seems to me that English teachers have to uphold some standards. The world is full of delicate clearances—like an airfield—and I value care and precision in language. I want my doctor to know the difference between tonsils and appendix when he operates on me, and if English teachers say students can use contractions and any other informal forms they choose, what happens to the delicate clearances of our language? We'll soon be crashing into one another.

As the discussion continues, the group and the change agent develop a clearer idea of individual attitudes toward language. Other issues that are useful for stimulating opening discussion include: A speaker should always avoid dialect; current changes in our language signify its degradation; when usage disputes present us with two or more alternatives, there is always one "preferred" choice; social acceptability in middle class society depends upon correct use of language.

Discussions have the advantage of airing many attitudes in a short time, but we don't think they are an ideal way to begin the change process because they may create false impressions. Often group participants withhold true feelings about language issues because they fear arousing displeasure within the group. Also, there is always the danger that a few people will dominate the discussion. Therefore, written and oral inventories are better. Written inventories can elicit thoughtful individual responses, while oral interviews produce more spontaneous views. As change agents, we have used oral questionnaires, meeting with each individual if possible, or assigning pairs who alternate roles of questioner-recorder and responder. Taken together, oral and written inventories provide a useful composite of the participants' attitudes toward many aspects of language.

Asking group members to respond to specific usages provides one kind of inventory, and the Appendix contains several usage scales which can be adapted. One of these is the "English Usage Questionnaire." This scale contains a few items of British usage which may not be appropriate for American groups, but the scale's attention to context (informal/formal, spoken/written) is an attribute which outweighs this slight limitation. Attention to the language situation, as in the "English Usage Questionnaire," fosters less monolithic attitudes toward language. Also in the Appendix is Leonard's "Current Usage in Grammar as Ranked by Linguists." Although developed before 1932, this scale has items which work well with contemporary groups. The three rankings—established, disputable, and illiterate—represent the reactions of professional writers and teachers surveyed some forty years ago. Items from all three categories can be combined in a single list which respondents can rate according to the same three criteria. A more lighthearted but nonetheless valuable inventory is "Quinn's Quiz," which draws items from famous published works to illustrate precedents for questionable contemporary usages. These scales, or adaptations of them, provide an assessment of the group's stance on usage generally, and discussion of particular items on the scales can lead to thoughtful exploration. Opinions on each item usually vary widely, and when participants explain judgments and exchange views, they begin to recognize inherent difficulties in absolute standards of usage.

To encourage group members to become more conscious of their assumptions about language, we often ask them to state the linguistic assumption that underlies a given statement. Formulating such assumptions is not a simple task, and it takes considerable probing to help participants articulate them. Often the initial statement is a variation of one of the language myths discussed in Chapter One. For example, a participant might respond negatively to the item "The engine was hitting good this morning" and defend that response by explaining that we shouldn't allow people to speak dialects. When pushed, the participant might go on to state the underlying assumption that dialects are undesirable forms of speech. The texts in which the "English Usage Questionnaire" and Leonard's "Current Usage in Grammar as Ranked by Linguists" appear contain extensive considerations of each usage item. We have found it effective to read excerpts from them when discussions become especially lively.

Language attitude inventories or opinionnaires offer another means of assessing group attitudes; the Appendix contains inventories by Frogner, Houston, and Taylor. Houston's "Language Attitudes and Information Study" investigates opinions about and knowledge of language learning; "Taylor's Language Attitude Scale" pays particular attention to attitudes toward nonstandard dialects. These and similar language attitude inventories help groups articulate their feelings about language and provide the basis for useful discussions. One liability of such scales is that they may elicit inaccurate responses. Since theory and practice do not always coincide, participants may respond as they think they should rather than with complete honesty.

Inventories that seek responses to actual or simulated language often elicit more genuine response and are therefore worth the inconvenience of making or obtaining audio tapes. We have used an audio tape similar to those used in Fraser's study (see note 3 of Chapter One). We use one tape of a speaker whose dialect is close to that of the audience and one of a speaker whose dialect suggests another region. Lexical and syntactic features can also be varied depending upon the group's linguistic background. For example, with an urban group familiar with Black English you might use this passage: "I done gone to the store most time and then one day I be busy and send Nick boy. He brung me what I tell him but he say somebody hit him upside the head and it don't be all his fault." Participants then record responses to this taped passage on forms such as this:

1. What is the race or ethnic origin of this speaker?
2. What is the highest educational level attained by this speaker?
3. What occupation might this speaker have?
4. Could this speaker be part of your social group?
5. Do you consider this speaker fluent?

A variation is to use rating scales based on two polar terms with three intermediate points: |̲̲̲̲̲|̲̲̲̲̲|̲̲̲̲̲|̲̲̲̲̲|. Other
               fast   slow

terms that may be used include clear/unclear, fluent/not fluent, relaxed/tense, high social status/low social status. Still another variation is to tape voices of children and ask group members (assuming they are all teachers) to rate the speaker's potential as a student. This can be done with narrative questions similar to 1-5 above or with polar terms such as confident/unsure, eager/reticent, intelligent/slow learner, precocious/retarded.

In a one-day workshop where the group will not have time to analyze responses fully, it may be desirable for participants to list the most pressing problems in student grammar, pronunciation, and vocabulary. As is true with open-ended discussion, this technique can lead to over-concentration on a few items or on one or two individuals in the group, making it difficult to direct the tide of teacher self-righteousness to more productive topics of discussion.

Investigating Curriculum Models

If the group is to meet for more than one day, a second, related set of attitudes should be investigated early in the discussion. In a general way these attitudes center on the nature of knowledge, but for purposes of teachers' groups they gel as curriculum models. Eggleston labels the ends of the curriculum continuum as *received* and *reflexive* perspectives. In his words, the received view of curriculum "is one in which the curriculum knowledge, like other components of the knowledge system in the social order, is accepted as a received body of understanding that is 'given,' even ascribed, and is predominantly non-negotiable."[5] A reflexive perspective, on the other hand, "is one in which curriculum knowledge, like the components of the knowledge system, is seen to be negotiable; in which content may be legitimately criticized and argued or new curricula devised. Essentially it is dialectic and manifestly subject to political and other influence; a construction of those who participate in its determination."[6] As an alternative to these two extremes Eggleston offers the *restructuring* perspective characterized by the following question: "How may the curriculum not only assist a wider range of students to enhance their expectations of power and their capacity to exercise it but also play its part in bringing about a social situation in which these expectations and capacities may be used?"[7]

If you consider the close relationship between language and power in society, the value of the restructuring perspective is evident. But our group discussions do not begin with the active consideration of this question. Rather, we try to engage teachers in discussions which reveal their preferred curriculum perspective and allow them to distinguish between their own attitudes and the structures or objective realities in which they work. For example, teachers may make narrative responses to statements such as: 1) Teachers are responsible for preserving the heritage of the past and handing it on to the next generation. 2) Students should have an active role in deciding what and how they will learn. 3) School curriculum should empower students by presenting them with situations which allow them to exercise power. Or their responses may be polar. For example, the language curriculum should: constantly change/never change, draw upon student dialects/ instruct students in approved forms of standard English, draw upon community resources/avoid contamination of corrupt public utterance.

Facilitating Group Awareness and Interest

As is true with discussion related to language attitude inventories, curriculum questions may elicit heated responses. Change agents should find these lively exchanges hopeful, even when they are difficult to facilitate, because they signal group involvement, and involvement leads to interest. It is important to acknowledge strong feelings about language and language teaching as they emerge; otherwise, group members tend to stop responding. Try to avoid taking stands, but encourage group members to criticize the statements of others. Take a nondirective approach, listening carefully to what is being said so that you can repeat it to the group, asking the speakers if this is an accurate reflection of what they've said. Open communication is essential in the awareness and interest stages of the change process, and an accepting atmosphere where all speakers get respectful recognition seems to foster such communication.

Of course there are times when smiling, nodding, and making accepting noises are not enough, since participants may need to vent their hostility. As attitudes emerge in more emotional terms, use more active means of restating them, perhaps through role playing. For example, an individual may begin by recounting the "unpleasant language" used by his/her students. With rapidly rising voice she or he exclaims, "I can't stand it when students say 'yeah' when I speak to them or when they say things like 'I ain't got no pencil.'" Suggest then that the speaker take the role of teacher while another group member plays the student. We suggest a variety of scenarios—teacher ignores student, teacher rebukes student, teacher offers alternative usage, teacher responds matter-of-factly to student statement. Ask both participants to explore their feelings about each alternative. As a follow-up we ask the two to reverse roles and replay the scenarios to learn how the other side feels.

Often, however, group members talk only in general terms about what bothers them; then the change agent's job is to steer conversation to a more specific level. Typical comments, especially at the beginning of group work, are generalities—students use terrible grammar, students can't write, students have limited vocabularies. Keep asking for examples until you begin to hear statements such as: "This one kid in my class keeps saying 'he gots' instead of 'he has'"; "When they are assigned a two-page composition, my students turn in one paragraph"; "Students keep inserting 'you know' after every third word."

When the group has begun to talk in more specific terms, encourage attitude statements or at least first-person statements. Offer examples and urge members to take responsibility for their own observations rather than to project them onto someone else. When members speak in the third person, ask them to restate in the first person and to add affective content whenever it is appropriate. Thus, "Students keep using 'anymore' the wrong way" becomes "I find it confusing when students say 'We eat fish here anymore,'" and "Students in this school have the most atrocious pronunciation" becomes "I don't like the flat â that many of my students use; they pronounce 'Ann' like 'Ian.'"

Because "I messages" are often difficult for teachers—and other people—to articulate, give group members opportunities to practice with one another. Working in pairs, participants express their three greatest concerns about language to their partners. The partner's job is to ensure that the statement is in the first person and to offer a restatement so that she or he can report it later to the group. After each partner has taken both roles, the first-person concerns are reported to the group.

These same strategies—listening carefully, remaining sensitive to group feelings, reiterating individual statements, using role playing for constructive expression of strong feeling, reducing global declarations to specific statements, encouraging first-person expression, and acknowledging individual feelings—are important throughout the entire change process, not just during the first couple of meetings. Our greatest failures have resulted when we truncated the process. Interactive skills, or relationship intervention as we called it in Chapter Two, are essential throughout the change process. Now let us move on to discuss other aspects of the process of change.

One of the advantages of asking group members to state concerns specifically is that change agents begin to discover the group's real needs. The ability of people to disclose themselves and their needs varies, but the typical pattern is for them to begin with generalities or peripheral concerns and work gradually to central needs. Asking for specifics leads to disclosure and makes group tasks clearer. We have learned, through painful experience, that group needs rather than the change agent's needs must determine much of the agenda, particularly at the outset. Our least successful encounters have resulted when we tried to work from an agenda and gave little attention to what the group was looking for. Typically, group needs take very pragmatic form: teachers want to know what to do, if not on Monday, then Tuesday. As change agents we try to strike a balance between this pressure for classroom strategies and our conviction that theory must underlie practice.

Although they are expressed in different ways, group concerns usually center on the need for answers; if the profession can't offer authoritative answers, teachers say, what can it give us? What can we tell our students and ourselves? Discrepancy intervention, or enlarging upon differences between group members and "experts" in the profession, is effective at this stage. Usage inventories provide ready examples of differences within the group, and perusal of the usage commentary in contemporary dictionaries reveals the differences in authoritative opinion. The 1976 edition of *The American Heritage Dictionary of the English Language,* for example, boasts of "exposing the lexical opinions of a larger group of recognized leaders than has heretofore been consulted so that the ordinary user, looking up an expression whose social status is uncertain, can discover just how and to what extent his presumed betters agree on what he ought to say or write."[8] This larger group of leaders is divided on many issues of usage. *Contact* (noun) denoting a person as a source of assistance is "acceptable to 61 percent of the Panel in formal usage."[9] What about the opinion of the other 39 percent? Are we to ignore them? What shall we do about "I felt bad" (regretful) which 55 percent of the panel will accept in speech? A brief examination of the history of the English language (another source for perspective intervention) adds to group awareness of shifting usages.

We urge group members to broaden their awareness of discrepancies in usage by reading W. H. Mittins, et al., *Attitudes to English Usage,* Cornelia and Bergen Evans's *A Dictionary of Contemporary American Usage,* Albert Marckwardt and Fred Walcott's *Facts About Current English Usage,* Charles C. Fries's *American English Grammar,* Robert Pooley's *The Teaching of English Usage,* Margaret Bryant's *Current American Usage,* and Ray Copperud's *American Usage: The Consensus.* These sources reflect both descriptive surveys and the compilers' attitudes. The group serves as a sounding board for individual reactions to these readings.

Group Projects

Keeping in mind the group's need for action as well as theory, encourage each member to undertake a project which will provide empirical information about language. Project designs vary depending upon interests and resources, but the aim is to make group members more conscious of usage in their immediate worlds. Typical projects suggest the range of possibilities: 1) focus upon the occurrence of selected "questionable" usages such as "finalize," "not about to" (determination not to do), "real" (as in "real cold"), and others suggested by the group, noting the frequency and context of each term; 2) monitor selected speakers—in the media and in person—for a week and note "questionable" usages in their speech; 3) monitor selected pages of a local newspaper—editorials, letters, advice columns, features, sports, and general news—and note linguistic choices of various kinds of writers; 4) survey community attitudes toward language by administering oral or written versions of the initial inventories to a sample of typical community members; 5) survey student attitudes with these same inventories, assuring students that their responses will not be used to evaluate them in class; 6) tape a typical conversation in a specialized work place such as an auto mechanic shop or attorney's office and play it to several listeners without revealing the setting; 7) tape several sentences by a speaker of nonlocal dialect, play it to speakers of local dialect, and record their reactions. A more extensive and highly satisfying project, if time allows, is for each group member to study the language of one child. Extensive conversation and tape recordings are essential for successful study, but the increased understanding of language justifies the effort. Projects which involve taping can start from a number of specific questions, such as: How does Speaker X's conversational language differ from "standard English"? Does Speaker X seem able to vary his or her dialect according to the communication situation? What particular characteristics of Speaker X's language make it effective/ineffective for particular communicative purposes?

Projects such as the ones listed above inevitably lead to increased awareness of the sociological dimensions of language and then to organizational/cultural structure intervention as described in Chapter Two. Sociolinguistics has, of course, added much to our understanding of the relationship between society and language, but assimilation of this knowledge is more likely to occur in combination with direct observation of language in society.

Developing group awareness of the impact of attitudes upon language and fostering interest in the topic is ongoing. Group members repeatedly confront their own and others' responses to language and begin to understand the impact their attitudes have upon their own classroom behavior and that of their students. As is true with relationship intervention, the growth of awareness and interest continues throughout the change process.

Evaluation

Evaluation begins as soon as alternatives appear. It may not be immediately apparent, but group members are usually making judgments, weighing alternatives, and considering their stances even as they respond to usage inventories. As they recognize that historical continuity rather than empirical validity accounts for many of their assumptions, they react in a variety of ways, some testifying to the difficulty and pain of change. As change agents we try to acknowledge this pain and at the same time encourage the group to consider alternatives to present practices. An equally possible reaction is relief—even delight—at not having to carry around the load of linguistic guilt and the fear of being wrong; change is a complicated process, but it is not always painful. Even if the group decides to maintain current practices, conscious examination assures more judicious practice. Try to sustain the group's awareness of alternatives through scanning rather than identification strategies: reading descriptions of programs, examining curriculum materials, and, if possible, visiting classrooms where new approaches are being implemented.

Extensive scanning and evaluation of alternatives to current language teaching leads to experimentation with new approaches. Once again, the group can serve as an effective testing ground. If the group has been meeting for some time, there may be a high enough level of trust so that members feel comfortable in taking risks with one another. We encourage them to develop and try mini-lessons which reflect changing attitudes toward language. A teacher may, for example, demonstrate a lesson on contextual meaning and solicit group response to the content and methodology.

Adoption/Adaptation

The final stage in the process is the adoption/adaptation of new procedures; however, in keeping with an adaptive rather than adoptive view of change, avoid thinking of this as a final stage. Change agents should encourage group members to try new approaches in their classes, especially when their efforts have been strengthened by experimentation within the group. These innovations might include teaching a unit on dialectology; banning the words "right" and "wrong" in reference to specific language choices except where each word is qualified by a situational reference; initiating frequent class discussions about assumptions that teacher and students reveal in their reactions to language; inviting other faculty members into their classes for participation in discussions about "correct" English; developing new criteria for the selection of language and composition textbooks; revising style sheets (or whatever criteria a department or school has agreed to use for writing); creating composition assignments that call for experimentation with several dialects; inviting teachers at other levels (senior high to elementary) to cooperate in revising expectations for student language. In any event, try to prevent the group from assuming that its task is over when the group ceases to meet regularly or after members have tried something new in their classes. If our methods are successful, group members will continue to challenge assumptions about language and language instruction, to examine new ideas, and to change.

We should emphasize, too, that the adoption/adaptation stage is often the most precarious time for participating teachers. They are taking risks in an often hostile environment (few schools are openly receptive to change) and may be asked to offer extensive explanations or defenses for their actions. Further, it is at this time that teachers experience the full psychological complexity involved in changing attitudes toward language because all three dimensions—affective, cognitive, and behavioral—converge. This convergence forces acknowledgement that their myths have changed.

Notes

1. Francis Bacon, *De Augmentis Scientiarum,* as quoted in Margery Purver, *The Royal Society: Concept and Creation* (London: Routledge & Kegan Paul, 1967), p. 53.
2. Orlando L. Taylor, "Teachers' Attitudes toward Black and Nonstandard English as Measured by the Language Attitude Scale," in *Language Attitudes,* ed. Roger W. Shuy and Ralph W. Fasold, p. 198.
3. Courtney B. Cazden, *Child Language and Education* (New York: Holt, Rinehart & Winston, 1972), p. 161.
4. George H. Gallup, "Eighth Annual Gallup Poll of the Public's Attitudes Toward the Public Schools," *Phi Delta Kappan* 58 (October 1976): 190.
5. John Eggleston, *The Sociology of the School Curriculum* (London: Routledge & Kegan Paul, 1977), p. 52.
6. Ibid.
7. Ibid., p. 71.
8. William Morris, ed., *The American Heritage Dictionary of the English Language* (Boston: Houghton Mifflin Co., 1976), pp. xxiii–xxiv.
9. Ibid., p. 287.

Scene: Same place, same group, different day

Burr: Whew, I'm glad we have Open House only once a year. I thought I was going to be eaten alive by some of the parents last night.

Motz: What do you mean? What happened?

Burr: You probably didn't get any of it because you teach history, but parents were on my neck about the "illiteracy" of kids in this school.

Carlucci: I guess we have the press to thank for that. Remember that series of articles in the *News* about changes in the English curriculum? Several parents asked me if that meant we don't teach writing anymore.

Schutz: Yes, and then there was the article on the standardized tests given by the state. According to the *News*, kids in this state can barely talk.

Brown: Am I ever glad I teach chemistry. None of the parents seem to know much about it, so they assume I know what I'm doing. You poor English teachers are always getting attacked. Why don't you start *doing* something about it?

Schutz: What do you have in mind? Reducing English to formulas and equations?

Carlucci: That's what transformational grammar does, I hear.

Brown: Don't be ridiculous. I wasn't thinking of drastic curriculum change so much as trying to establish a different relationship to the community, helping groups in the community explore their attitudes toward language. You seem to want to avoid getting cynical and defensive. Why don't you try coming up with some ways to be a positive influence on the community's attitudes as well as on the kids'?

Motz: You're implying change of a pretty fundamental kind. That NCTE statement that Liz quoted a few days ago has haunted me. I know enough history to realize that when you start consciously trying to mess around with a community's beliefs, you're playing with fire. "An attempt of one social group to exert its dominance over another": that's political, ladies and gentlemen, and I counsel caution.

Brown: Yes, I suppose I am suggesting something that's potentially dangerous, but I think we've got some teachers here who can handle it. They certainly know you can't go on a rampage with hobby-horse ideas and expect to win converts.

Schutz: Ellen, Joe, I think you're both right. We English teachers have reached the point where we understand enough about language and attitudes and change processes to try to go beyond the school walls. We've never really done it before, but I'm coming to think it's really a part of our jobs. Somehow, we've got to talk to the community about the ways that language affects them, but we can't sound like zealots. Sue, Frank, what do you say?

4 Changing Language Attitudes in the Community

English is a subject which nearly everyone agrees is vital for effectively functioning citizens in a democracy: everyone needs to be able to communicate with fluency, precision, and as much grace as possible, and English teachers are supposed to develop that ability. But teaching students to communicate effectively with language is only a vague statement of purpose and content for English teachers. The real question for teachers is how to do it, and there is professional disagreement about procedures. While it may be unfortunate that the public persists in its conviction that English teachers are the authorities on how language should be used, at least that belief gives English teachers a leverage that belongs to no other group in the community. When English teachers speak to the community about language, a large portion of the community will listen.

Thoughtful and imaginative English teachers maintain a delicate balance between "practical" instruction in language use and those dimensions of language that give aesthetic delight and suggest explorations of values. These teachers are more thoroughly knowledgeable about language from descriptive, rhetorical, and literary standpoints and, as Arthur Applebee has shown in *Tradition and Reform in the Teaching of English,* they have drawn from several literary traditions and from "scientific" schools of thought.[1] They have become synthesizers and explorers in their attempts to make English enriching beyond, but not excluding, the more immediate and perhaps mundane uses of language in daily life. Such teachers have truly been educators of the larger community. Their students do not perpetuate the stultifying and rigid attitudes toward language that their parents inherited. Rather, their students demonstrate that an enlightened understanding of language contributes to fluency and comfort with language in everyday affairs.

As English teachers, we like to think that we are making an important difference in people's lives if we are successful in helping our students to be more thoughtful and more sensitive. Such a goal is, however, as general as it is important and thus impels us to take a closer look at more specific and direct influences that English teachers can have on their communities. Obvious targets for change are those beliefs about language that are called myths in Chapter One. English teachers might try working more directly in the community, finding ways to disseminate their knowledge about language through existing avenues of community instruction. A community *does* instruct itself through its available means of communication, from conversation to television and advertising. Since an expanded concept of English instruction includes all these media, we must stop just *teaching* these concepts and start *employing* them. This doesn't mean anything so conspicuous or shocking as having a zealous teacher lecture on linguistic relativism right after the six o'clock news. That approach is both too direct and too likely to alienate the community. Indeed, in whatever we say and in whatever means we use, we will need to seek community support. As politics makes clear, the leader cannot be too far ahead of those who would follow. But we can redefine our roles as teachers of language and as teachers of the communities in which we live.

An Active Community Role

This new role for English teachers is characterized more by its *active* than its *reactive* nature. Recent questioning and accusations about the imputed weaknesses in students' reading and writing skills have elicited defensive reactions from English teachers and other school personnel. English teachers, asserting that they have been teaching basic skills all along, have even resurrected and revised sentence diagramming. Another kind of reaction occurred in the 1960s when elective programs proliferated, often in response to the students' complaints that English had become too rigid and irrelevant. One conclusion might be that we English teachers are intensely political in our statements about our field, if not in our public behavior. We can adjust our purpose and our methods to whatever breeze is strongest. Another conclusion, perhaps more valid and certainly more damaging, is that too many of us have not clearly and thoroughly established our sustaining beliefs and assumptions. We often do not articulate our beliefs in a departmental philosophy or network of assumptions about language. Instead, we disagree and bicker, choking on gnats of usage, defending idiosyncratic style preferences. Such divisiveness and the absence of a coherent statement of beliefs about language leave us vulnerable and force us to take a reactive stance when the community becomes upset.

An active stance with respect to language and the community can arise from allowing our own attitudes to undergo change, radically (in the sense of going to the roots) rethinking the roles of schools and teachers in the communities they serve. This is not the place for a thorough analysis of the historical and philosophical development of American schools, but we can look to John Dewey as a thinker whom many of us will agree did perform such an analysis. In *Democracy and Education,* Dewey describes American education as preeminently a social function; the school provides a special environment created to perform a major part of that function. This special environment is "framed with express reference to influencing the mental and moral disposition" of the members of a given community.[2] Carrying out that influence, again according to Dewey, entails three characteristic functions:

1. The school breaks up the complex interrelationships of a society and orders them in simplified and progressive ways. "It selects the features which are fairly fundamental and capable of being responded to by the young." This selection and ordering of elements becomes a "means of gaining insight into what is more complicated."

2. In addition to simplifying, selection of features of the existing environment aims "at weeding out what is undesirable ... it strives to reenforce the power of ... only such [achievements] as make for a better future society." This is the principle of offering to the young the best that a society has produced.

3. The school also acts as an integrating and balancing agent within a society of many centrifugal forces. If modern society is "many societies more or less loosely connected," then some institution is needed which "shall provide something like a homogeneous and balanced environment for the young." This influence counteracts the antagonistic pulls of the diverse social groups which affect the child—a danger according to Dewey—and the school performs "a steadying and integrating office."[3]

This description of function obviously places schools at the core of any community, both as responsible preservers of a heritage and as agents for improvement. The difficulty of keeping these two purposes in flexible harmony is apparent to any careful observer of twentieth-century American schools. Tension between the two functions seems clearly desirable, but a productive tension is difficult to sustain and often the temptation is to settle for an easy resolution. It is easier to opt for the familiar, the continuity of old ways and ideas, regardless of whether they can be shown to be "the best" or the most productively integrative. Without cleareyed and continual internal reassessment by school personnel, the deadening influence of precedent can be strongest, and the school becomes a captive of the community rather than a leader in it. With captivity comes timidity; with timidity, sameness and little genuine innovation.

Doubtless, examples exist here and there of schools that have sought an energetic and innovative balance between preservation and change, between reaction and action. One of them is described in lively detail by Polly Greenberg in *The Devil Has Slippery Shoes*.[4] This "biased biography of the Child Development Group of Mississippi" traces the development of a preschool program created with federal funds and the genuine participation of blacks in spite of the intense opposition of many local whites. The author sums up the purpose of the program with these words:

> It was hoped that at least a small group of Negro children, who had already had the tremendous advantage of having parents who were engaged in changing things, could get a psychologically strengthening, thought provoking, reality oriented education, rather than the psychologically crushing, thought controlled, mythically oriented education currently available to them in public schools.[5]

CDGM was funded for about a year, intermittently, and managed to develop alternative educational services for several hundred black children. But it did not confine itself to youngsters. Staff and involved black citizens worked with other community action programs, such as adult literacy and economic opportunities, to combat the poverty and degradation in which most blacks lived. "Surely one of the most important things CDGM did for Mississippi, for the South, was to provide an arena for emerging newstyle Southern white leaders."[6] One of them, the Reverend Jimmy Jones, born and raised in the Delta town of Leland, Mississippi, said:

> In the last analysis, no individual has to be a victim of anything. Each of us makes a decision. . . . History doesn't just make itself. Somebody gets an idea from the mesh he's in, and he moves out alone with his idea and he educates himself and others and forms a model that's back down in the mesh; but it's *new*. The perpetual revolution is what I see as the essence of life. The job will never be done by people who do something and then sit back down and never do anything else—or people who never do anything at all. I call them the living dead. An idea is like any living

thing: the minute it's birthed, it's on its way to death. We have to keep on with the birthing process—creating, creating, learning, experimenting. ...[7]

But one of the most significant comments about the whole effort, and the one that best suggests the author/participant's view of its nature and effects, was from "a large lady from Lauderdale County":

> 'Course CDGM's good. 'Cept the things about it that's bad. There's a lotta good folks come here to help us. 'Course, there's a lot just come to cause a fuss too. And the federal government's finally recognized us down here—'course sometimes that ain't so good, 'cause for every smile it gives us, it gives us a kick too. Well, at least it's got us colored peoples workin' for oursel's. 'Cept the ones that won't. One thing, though, it's great for the kids. On'y thing, it's kinda hard on 'em when they get to real school and it ain't like our school. God's helpin' us, ain't no doubt. It's just that the Devil keeps skippin' in and outa things so's we won't get spoilt. He really keeps you guessin'! Each thing, you gotta study it to see if it's God in the disguise of difficulty, or the Devil in the disguise of somebody good. This whole thing really keep us workin' our mind.[8]

CDGM is not a literal model for change in a community, but it does demonstrate the possibility of significant attitude change in the face of massive resistance, and it beckons the Jimmy Joneses who happen to be English teachers to help with the birthing of new attitudes. It is a specific example of the Dewey principle in action: a school weeding out the undesirable and moving actively toward the creation of a better society.

We English teachers who aspire to be Jimmy Joneses need to reevaluate our capacities and community roles. A good way to begin is to imagine a career change. We've come to a point in our careers where we realize that we must inventory our skills, desires, and experiences in order to find a new job or to make our present job more satisfying. Sometimes this stock-taking is forced upon us by reversals in the supply and demand market for teachers; sometimes we do it simply to avoid stagnation. If that reassessment is done probingly and imaginatively, as Richard Bolles explains in *What Color Is Your Parachute?*,[9] it can turn up a variety of talents and skills that have surprisingly wide application. It can also reinforce a spirit of confidence about our potential effectiveness outside our classrooms, and that spirit can be very helpful when "the Devil keeps skippin' in and outa things."

Many good English teachers have superior communicative ability, an ability to write in several forms (expository, fiction, verse) and for a variety of audiences. Like Jimmy Jones, they can look at miscellaneous events, find the patterns that underlie them, and succinctly express their significance. This is the ability to deal comfortably with an idea without being so bewitched by it that it becomes dogma. English teachers are accustomed to helping groups solve problems, explore opinions, and propose courses of action. Our own efforts as organizers and facilitators of student work have helped us develop a remarkable range of group dynamics skills. In addition to working with people, we have organized and directed the use of communications equipment: projectors, tape recorders, typewriters, duplicating machines. We have helped to publish newspapers and magazines, which even entailed coping with budgets and the whims of advertisers. If we have had to explain and defend the choice of books whose suitability was in question or if we have had to argue for an English department's priorities in the face of administrative opposition, we have employed persuasive tactics. In other words, many English teachers have multicolored parachutes which could be more fully deployed if we learned to manipulate the cords in different ways.

Access to the Community

And what of the "mesh" we're in, the community? What unsuspected or only partially tapped resources is it likely to contain? Perhaps an informal survey (with the Yellow Pages and Chamber of Commerce materials as starting points) will produce a list similar to this:
- at least one local radio station which reaches a large proportion of the community or, if there are several radio stations, one which has a targeted audience (youth, blacks, intellectuals, middle-class adults). Each of these audiences has a different perception of "normal" language, which will suggest to a change agent different approaches to affecting language attitudes
- at least one television station in or serving the community, which by the terms of its FCC license is committed to some public service programming
- at least one daily or weekly newspaper to which access is possible through letters to the editor and through editorials and feature stories
- businesses and industries that regularly advertise their products or services, whose ad language might be influenced or whose advertising departments might be convinced to include messages about language in the ads

- house organs of businesses and industries which communicate all sorts of messages to employees
- in-house workshops and seminars conducted by businesses and industries, sometimes in connection with problems of communication
- advertising agencies that create and market messages to the public in such places as newspapers, magazines, TV, radio, billboards, product packaging
- governmental offices and agencies whose regular function is to provide services to the public and which have many communication tools for that purpose
- churches whose pastoral care includes attention to the influences of language on behavior
- a public library, which is the natural repository for cognitive information
- service and social clubs whose members may have narrow criteria for membership but who may also want to expand their interests and understanding.

These are the means by which a community instructs itself, and English teachers either are or could be a part of all of them, influencing some of the instruction they provide. And, of course, tapping their devices of communication is the way to do that. Into the mesh that is these organizations' habitual way of thinking and behaving must be inserted the new ideas Jimmy Jones spoke of, the new ideas that will only momentarily seem new and then will be absorbed in the continual growth process. The stages of change that we have cited in the previous chapters will apply here too, with the major emphasis on creating awareness of different attitudes toward language.

Activities for Change Agents

Individually, and sometimes collectively, English teachers have already acted as change agents in some communities. Marge Huntley is a good example of the solitary change agent. An English teacher with fifteen years of experience, she lives and teaches in a community of 25,000, a fairly typical community whose residents include industrial workers, professional people, and clerical and service personnel. Marge teaches in a senior high school where she has served as English department chairperson but is now a classroom teacher. She took part in an NDEA Institute in the mid-1960s, as an NCTE member, and has helped with various activities of the state affiliate of NCTE. These kinds of participation, supplemented, of course, by reading in professional books and periodicals, have made her somewhat more alert to the many points of growth in a teacher of English than some of her colleagues.

Marge likes to write, and she is not hesitant to use this ability in public ways. Readers of the editorial page in the local newspaper are accustomed to seeing her name there. She writes about many aspects of education, but usually she tries in some way to include references to the functions of language. One letter about standardized testing, for example, pointed out that such tests make some possibly unwarranted assumptions about dialects. She drew an analogy with clothing, asking, "Would you wear the same suit of clothes for all occasions? Of course not. Then, why must we assume that certain language forms are suitable for all occasions? If standardized tests are going to be important measures of our students' language facility, shouldn't we acknowledge that they assess only a small part of their and our range of choices?"

Because Marge regularly writes letters and because her views are always provocative and thoughtfully prepared, the editor of the newspaper asked her whether she would like to write a guest editorial. (Furthermore, he offered her $25 for 600 words!) Within a week she had written and sent off an essay which was printed the following week. The editor chose to highlight one passage by printing it in large type: "To try to defend certain choices of verb and pronoun forms by invoking a grammatical rule is to assume some inherent rightness for that rule. Grammar has no such rightness." In the last paragraph she summarized her argument thus: "English is a flexible instrument. All of us need to know more about how that instrument works, how it can be used to find and express meanings, how it can add satisfaction to our efforts to communicate. Changing our beliefs and attitudes about what is ungrammatical is a first, important step toward greater mastery of our language."

Marge continues to write, even though some of her colleagues regard her views and her techniques of expression as eccentric. Most of her students, however, speak glowingly of her. They refer to their enthusiastic discussions about language, and most of them seem to have emerged from her classes with a new appreciation of the flexibility inherent in language. It also seems that it is mainly her students' reactions that keep Marge going. So far as her colleagues and other adults are concerned, she is indeed a solitary change agent. One wonders how long she can sustain the energy for contributing to changed attitudes.

In communities where there are colleges or universities, the Department of English is sometimes the home of solitary change agents whose medium is the telephone. One such department known to us averages three calls a week from people inquiring about the "correctness" of some item of usage. A typical question is, "Which word should I use in this sentence: 'You asked that the regional director and *(I, me, myself)* determine the relative priorities.'" This question was answered by one of the secretaries in the English office, a woman who had been a public school English teacher; she could explain not only the "right" choice—*I*—but also the fact that formal, written English has different criteria for choice than informal, spoken English. That secretary, another solitary change agent, may have made a small contribution to changing attitudes toward language.

Roy Johnson, Jim Stevens, and Jeff Jones are the Three Musketeers of language attitude change in a large city. All three are secondary school English teachers whose loose but durable affiliation includes frequent thank-God-it's-Friday sessions at convenient taverns. They have worked with the state and local NCTE affiliates, but several of their activities are self-sponsored. That way they avoid some of the hassles and delays that accompany "official" positions by organizations with images to protect.

Almost every year, Roy, Jim, and Jeff have their classes do an interviewing project. With their kids, they devise questions for telephone interviews. They have found that political campaign managers have helpful suggestions about how to do interviewing— designing the questions, selecting a sample, conducting the interview—and, of course, they involve as many kids as possible in seeing the project through. The kids tabulate the answers, interpret the results, and try to pull them together with reading about dialects and style. But besides the obvious pedagogical value of this project, the three men discuss the myths about language that the interviews uncover and try to discern ways in which they can change those myths.

One myth that they worked on recently involves spelling. The interviews had shown a predominant belief that correct spelling is an indispensable criterion of effective written composition; furthermore, one of the local newspapers persisted in sponsoring city-wide spelling bees, which seemed to contribute substantially to exaggerated attention to spelling. Having spent several Friday afternoons in planning a strategy, Roy, Jim, and Jeff arranged a conference with the newspaper publisher and some of his staff. A result of that conference and subsequent correspondence and telephone calls was a shift in the newspaper's sponsorship. They decided to sponsor a young writers' fair instead, an annual sharing time on a college campus where elementary and secondary students from many schools could come together to read each other's work and to listen to adult writers talk about how they write.

It's too early to say that the community's belief in the spelling myth has been shaken, and the three young men know they will have to use additional strategies. One of them is directed at service and social clubs. Roy and Jim have friends who belong to Rotary, Kiwanis, and Lions; Jeff's wife knows people who are members of Soroptimist and University Women's Club. All of them have been informally urging their friends to suggest a program featuring language. One program idea is a forum about language. The plan is to invite a sportswriter, a newspaper editor, a businessperson, and a teacher. In modified debate form, they will compare their beliefs about language standards. They will use lots of examples and will refer to such benchmarks of judgment as Strunk and White, Chicago *Manual of Style*, custom, and the recent Supreme Court judgment about "dirty words" in the media. As Jeff, Roy, and Jim describe it, this appears to be the kind of program that can be extremely stimulating, and, if one of them can be the teacher participant in each debate, they hope to make the point that the myth of absolute criteria in language needs revision.

Another ad hoc group of teachers has built its activity largely around publications from NCTE, especially those produced by SLATE (Support for the Learning and Teaching of English, an arm of NCTE that is especially aimed at political action). They have duplicated some of the "Starter Sheets" (such as "Back to Basics: Language and Dialect," "Back to Basics: Grammar and Usage") and have distributed them at PTA and school board meetings. They included their names, addresses, and telephone numbers with these handouts and now get inquiries from interested citizens; some just want to chat, others suggest slightly more formal conversations with groups of parents of preschoolers, scout troop leaders, and the like. The teachers who participate in these discussions have a chance to raise questions about what is "basic" in language learning, and, because the people who attend are usually very interested in young people's development, the teachers find attentive listeners.

These same teachers have also nudged their school district and the local English teachers' organization into sponsoring public meetings on the subject of testing. They informed themselves both by studying the language portions of widely used standardized tests and the NCTE document, *Reviews of Selected Published Tests in English*. For use at the meetings they duplicated portions of another NCTE publication, *Common Sense and Testing in English:* "Checklist for Evaluating English Tests and Test Uses" and "Citizen's Edition: Common Sense and Testing in English." Among the questions that the "Citizen's Edition" encourages is the following: "Do the tests discriminate against children because they do not speak a particular type of English or because they come from a particular part of the United States?" Because there are numerous migrant workers whose children attend schools in this particular community, teachers have found this question almost explosive in its effect. Despite some ugly expressions of prejudice and ethnic hostility, the discussions can usually be brought around to focus on the arbitrariness of many school and test criteria. It now begins to appear that other forms of evaluation will replace the once-dominant standardized tests and that more tolerance for linguistic diversity may be growing among school personnel and some parents.

In still another medium-sized community, Sally Maclellan, a fourth-grade teacher, and Marie Steele, librarian in charge of the learning resource center, discovered that they had been similarly affected by Robert Pooley's *Teaching English Usage* (first published in 1946 by NCTE; a second edition, 1974, has also been published by NCTE). They recalled how fresh and sensible Pooley's reassurances about "errors" were when they first read them, though twenty-five years later some of his statements, they had to admit, seemed quaint. ("Unfortunate is the child who develops within the influence of substandard English. He not only forms bad habits of speech in the most impressionable years of his childhood, but he also reinforces these bad habits by countless repetitions prior to the influence of school.") Sally and Marie recognized that for a large portion of the adults in their community Pooley's 1946 attitudes were still operative. This gave them the idea of working out an arrangement with the public library for displays of special collections of books and articles. Some of the owners of local stores—including the book store—allowed the use of their windows for occasional displays. One display featured the word *ain't;* it showed that the word *is* "in the dictionary"— the venerable *Oxford English Dictionary,* as well as most modern ones—and that the word is unacceptable to some people only for social reasons, not because of matters of clarity or grammar. The display also directed the viewer's attention to materials at the public library that further clarify matters of usage.

Sally and Marie's method for changing language attitudes capitalizes on curiosity and does not require meetings or an initiating impulse from the community to be effective. Its advantages are simplicity and surprise. And with the cooperation of the public librarian, follow-up information, while it does not reach as many people as the display, is less likely to stay buried and relatively inaccessible.

For English teachers to expand their roles and to become educators of the community obviously requires time, which most English teachers lack. It is clearly not possible to teach four or five classes a day and also meet with community groups. Therefore, we propose that teachers begin helping administrators and school boards to rethink the English teacher's role.

One argument might go as follows: A frequent target of community criticism is the reading and writing skills of students. This criticism is often spurred by media accounts of widespread illiteracy, declining standardized test scores, and employer dissatisfaction with employee language skills. Since this criticism is usually based on slender evidence and misunderstandings about the nature of language learning processes, the schools will be better able to reply convincingly and develop conditions for more effective language learning if the community is better informed about language. Furthermore, informing people about so complex a subject is not simply a matter of handing out a fact sheet or holding one or two public meetings; better community understanding will come only from a prolonged and carefully designed series of educative efforts. Therefore, English teachers, as the best qualified spokespersons for language learning, need to be released from some of their current teaching duties in classrooms to work with segments of the community. Such use of teacher time is much more than public relations work; it binds school and community in a way that is at least as important as athletic, dramatic, and musical performances.

If this argument is persuasive to the school board, funds may be assigned specifically for several English teachers to work part-time with the community throughout the year. It may also be possible for the administration and school board to make a financial arrangement with local businesses or industries to support this work. To win the support of private executives, English teachers will need both long-range arguments and immediate, specific plans. The former can center on the widely accepted principle that a healthy democratic community needs highly literate people and that literacy is not acquired once and for all in public schools.

The argument can also develop the idea that several American corporations have begun to see their public service role in a much more comprehensive and integrated way; not only do they provide products and services, make profits for stockholders, and pay taxes, but they also ally themselves directly with community agencies that help to make the community culturally and ecologically healthy. Language, it can be shown, plays a significant part in preserving and improving this network of relationships.

At this point, we speculate about one access to the community that English teachers have seldom if ever used. Could we use the techniques and media of advertisers? Could we put a message about language attitudes into the advertiser's mode? We might begin by thinking along these lines: "I know what my message is. How can I convey it simply, with appeals to the emotions or the self-interest of the consumer, and with maximum memorability?" The resulting idea might be sketched out like this:

> A prevailing myth has it that standard English is a clearly definable set of correct pronunciations, grammatical structures, and word choices. We want to refashion this myth into one that acknowledges the variety within standard English, particularly in its spoken forms. We will use the sixty-second television spot announcement. Our central image, the equivalent of "standard," will be a suit of armor, an inflexible spine, a ruler, or a chest of drawers with labels for its contents. A voice-over will equate that image with "proper English." This image will then be superimposed on snatches of conversation spoken by several attractive people, each of whom uses different "accents," grammatical structures, and vocabulary levels. As each speaker appears and speaks, the superimposed image explodes or blurs. If needed, the voice-over concludes the sequence with a statement like, "Proper English has many forms."

Strange as such a technique may seem to English teachers, it does acknowledge the affective, nonrational elements of myth. If we limit our educational procedures to appeals of "fact" and "logic," we are likely to ignore some of the most powerful shaping forces and modes of community instruction. This exercise in thinking visually about ideas related to language can acquaint us with the notion that there are new ways to gain access to the public consciousness. With a few such ideas, teachers can go to a local television station with the proposal that some public service time be devoted to language. Details of scripting and production would of course have to be left to the television specialists, but teachers could offer advice on transforming the ideas into transmittable images and words.

Advertisers and advertising agencies might also respond positively to ideas about incorporating certain language themes in their copy. For example, perhaps the idea that spelling and pronunciation are supposed to correspond closely (e.g., *gonna* = going to? *hafta* = have to?) could be explored in a series of game-like inserts in product advertising. (Breakfast cereal boxes would seem one obvious place.) Using some of the variants of phoneme-grapheme relationships that have emerged from recent computer analyses of English, the games could establish both the lack of close fit and the idea that variation in spelling need not be a reason for extreme discomfort or pejorative judgment. English teachers could supply the appropriate linguistic information and suggestions for the games to the advertisers and could urge them to place the games on packaging materials or even billboards.

In a similar vein, some companies, especially public utilities, might agree to print brochures to include with their bills. "We all speak dialects" is one possible theme for such an insert. The same message, phrased with different vocabulary and syntactical choices, could be presented with the overall reminder that each version is acceptable for a particular occasion and that no way is best for all occasions.

Approaching a company with this sort of suggestion could be a good way to arouse the curiosity of the company staff. Surprised that these English teachers don't conform to a stereotyped role, staff members may want to sit down and discuss with the English teacher-change agent these new ideas. Such a discussion might lead to an exploration of policies about language that are current within that company. What role do certain standards of language have in the world of business? Are possibly archaic usages demanded in correspondence and reports? If the discussion reveals that certain beliefs need reassessment in the light of recent linguistic information, the English teacher could suggest a workshop for company personnel. The company may be willing to pay for the released time of the teacher to conduct the workshop, or the teacher may be able to recommend someone to perform that service. Though workshops would probably not be aimed at immediate change in company policies regarding language, they can raise significant questions. Again, role playing is one of the best ways to introduce situations where judgments about language choices are brought into play and where the purpose is to examine the basis for judgment.

Several of the awareness strategies we have suggested, since they put English teachers into direct contact with the community, can lead to advanced stages in the change process—developing more intense interest, trial and evaluation, and adoptive/adaptive change. Steve Bolton, a high school English teacher, found that his church was a suitable place to achieve such focus. Working with the staff person for adult activities, he was able to schedule a series of consciousness-raising meetings. The invitations to church members noted that many instances of social injustice are perpetrated through language; bias based on sex or age, racial slurs, and vocational exclusion stem from archaic beliefs about language. Steve had collected numerous specific examples, which he shared with the group during six sessions and to which he encouraged group members to react. The group included vocational counselors, businesspeople, and others who worked with people from many segments of society. As they scanned the various attitudes implicit in these samples of linguistic behavior, they were able to assess the effects of alternate behavior. Steve believed that several of them were well on their way to adaptive change and would probably become positive influences on attitude in parts of that community.

Steve's approach involved a pre-existing organizational structure —the church congregation—but ad hoc groups are also possible, especially if they seem to offer something a little bit special. Sally Maclellan and Marie Steele followed up their bond with the public library by helping to organize a noncredit class, "Victims of Language," with the cooperation of the continuing education division of a local college. Publicity for the class asserted that most of us are unknowing victims of our own and others' language, that we create unnecessary traps for ourselves, and that one route to a happier and more productive life is to stop being a victim of language. The class attracted twelve people who met weekly with a library staff member who acted as coordinator and discussion leader. Because of the tie with the college, the class had the services of a college professor, one who knew that lectures were not called for in that setting and who served as resource person. With background in modern linguistics and psychology, she was able to provide the group with examples of language behavior and to encourage scanning. She and the discussion leader were careful not to make dogmatic assertions about the need to change attitudes; instead, they persistently encouraged examination of apparent victimization of people in their jobs and other social relationships. Negative examples related to responses like "poor grammar," "lazy speech," and "sloppy use of the English language" were interspersed with positive examples, many of which featured the ways we can and do play with language. (A recent book by Don and Alleen Pace Nilsen, *Language Play: An Introduction to Linguistics,* Newbury House, 1978, contains many such examples in the form of activities for individuals and groups.) These excursions into play helped to show that poetry and much literature are ways of pushing out the frontiers of language, that dialects reflect healthy diversity in language rather than decay, and that each one of us, with our own idiolect, can contribute something new and interesting. If the members of the class entered as victims of language, they emerged as active appreciators of the unexpectedly broad limits of language.

The preceding examples depict English teachers as agents of change in communities—not the kind of agents who make headlines or are conspicuous leaders, but rather agents who are alert to possible sources of influence. These sources often include existing organizations and resources, used in new and imaginative ways. As such teachers increase their own alertness to the changing attitudes toward language, they become active participants in the changing of those attitudes that do so much to shape our culture. "We have to keep on with the birthing process": the birthing of healthier attitudes.

Notes

1. Arthur N. Applebee, *Tradition and Reform in the Teaching of English: A History* (Urbana, Ill.: NCTE, 1974).
2. John Dewey, *Democracy and Education* (New York: The Free Press, 1944), p. 19.
3. Ibid., pp. 20–22.
4. Polly Greenberg, *The Devil Has Slippery Shoes* (London: Macmillan, 1969).
5. Ibid., p. 4.
6. Ibid., pp. 670–71.
7. Ibid., p. 671.
8. Ibid., p. xv.
9. Richard Nelson Bolles, *What Color Is Your Parachute?* (Berkeley, Calif.: Ten Speed Press, 1972).

Scene: Teachers' lounge in mid-May

Motz: I'm finishing off the year with a unit on myths—having the kids look at some of the relationships between myth and history.

Carlucci: Greek myths? I do them in my tenth grade literature class. Why are you doing them too? Aren't history teachers supposed to be more interested in facts?

Motz: It's not a question of either/or—facts *or* imagination. I'm trying to have the kids examine differing accounts of how our cultural beliefs and traditions developed. It seems like a good way to round off a year of world history—a synthesizer.

Schutz: That sounds very interesting to me. What are some of the myths you've used?

Motz: Well, we started with some Greek creation myths—Hesiod mostly—and of course the Genesis story.

Burr: Wow, that sounds risky. Will this community stand for calling Genesis a myth?

Motz: If anyone asks, I can explain that well enough. You see, I'm carefully developing the idea that myths are not necessarily untrue. They don't have to have empirical scientific backing to make them either credible or persuasive.

Brown: Oh? Tell me more. I believe science is the route to truth about the physical world at least. I'm skeptical about claiming that a scientifically validated cosmology theory is no better than a fanciful story about the origins of the universe.

Motz: Precisely. You point to the main reason that the concept of myth is so complicated and fascinating. Science presents its findings—its measurements, its verified hypotheses, and so on—as truth. But it is an "objective truth," something separate from emotions, not obviously relevant to people's everyday lives. Myth, though, goes beyond science and points out how natural phenomena have a bearing on the people who hear the myth. Take the Genesis myth: the notion that God created the world in six days has been reassuring to millions of people throughout the ages. It made an often frightening and hostile environment seem more comprehensible. It presented a benevolent and omnipotent deity who created a habitat especially for humans. Do you see how belief in that myth can be more reassuring and satisfying than a "factual" scientific explanation, at least at some stages of human evolution?

Schutz: Sure. That's "subjective truth." Very much a part of the literary experience. Feelings and intuitions are another level of understanding beyond the merely literal or factual. Joe, I'm delighted you're trying to get at that through history.

Motz: Well, you know how hard I try to help the kids see that history is not just a series of dates and dry accounts of battles and politics. I plan to end this unit with a look at John F. Kennedy and Martin Luther King. I hope they'll see that recent historical facts have already become elements of myth and that myth is more than fact.

Burr: My God, Joe, you're flipping all kinds of switches in my mind. I'm beginning to realize how compartmentalized my thinking has been. I've put factual history into one slot, imaginative literature in another, everyday language skills in another, and so on. The way you talk about myth suggests connections among all these things.

Brown: I'm seeing that too, Frank. I'm afraid I've assumed that science is the bedrock of truth about the world and that all other knowledge somehow has to be grounded in it.

Motz: Don't mistake me, now. I'm not saying that science is antagonistic to myth. As I said before, it's not either/or. But I do see science and history as helping to build and modify myths. It's a constant but usually slow process of revising myths so that they incorporate whatever seem to be facts with the human need for a system of values and beliefs.

Schutz: So all this talk we've been having about language attitudes fits into what you're saying about myth, doesn't it, Joe? We've been asking each other what we believe about language standards and why we teach certain language forms in our classes. And every time we've come up against the lack of any absolute standard. We've been forced to see language as embedded in social values.

Carlucci: Yes, I'll have to admit that even I can't be quite so sure as I was last September that I always know what is "right" in language. Now that I've tried to tell the rest of you some of my assumptions, I see how endless the process is. Every assumption seems to be tied to another one. Unless I'm just going to forget all this, I'll have to keep on questioning.

Motz: Isn't that one of the healthiest things we can do? The more immersed in history I've become and the more I recognize people's need through the ages for myths that both explain and satisfy, the more respect I have for questioning. It constantly challenges the myths and helps us to modify them so that they better suit our needs.

Brown: That reminds me of what Gertrude Stein said near the end of her life. She was summing up all she had learned about living. First she said, "What are the answers?" No one could tell her. Then she said, "What are the questions?" And she left it at that. We've got to try to figure out the right questions to ask.

Schutz: It seems to me we've got a good start on asking the right questions about language. Let's all try to get the same planning period next year. We've got a lot more talking to do.

Appendix

English Usage Questionnaire

Check one box in right hand columns for each numbered item.

	Informal		Formal	
	Speech	Writing	Speech	Writing
1. He did not do *as* well as the experts had expected.				
2. The audience was *very* amused.				
3. The conservative-minded are averse *to* making any changes.				
4. Traditional and *contemporary* furniture do not go well together.				
5. The data *is* sufficient for our purpose.				
6. The members of the team laughed at *each other*.				
7. We *have got* to finish the job.				
8. Young girls do not dress *the way* their grandmothers did.				
9. *Under* these circumstances no-one should complain.				
10. He is in London, but his family *are* in Bournemouth.				
11. The agreement *between* the four powers was cancelled.				
12. Answer *either* Question 1 *or* Question 2 *or* both.				
13. It was not *all that* easy.				
14. They will send the poultry *providing* the tax is low.				
15. The performance ended early, *due to* illness among the players.				

	Informal		Formal	
	Speech	Writing	Speech	Writing
16. We *met up with* him at the Zoo.				
17. The instruments were *pretty* reliable.				
18. There were *less* road accidents this Christmas than last.				
19. Competitors should try *and* arrive in good time.				
20. The process is *very unique*.				
21. He is older than *me*.				
22. They work *evenings* and *Sundays*.				
23. They behaved differently at school *than* they did at home.				
24. He *only had* one chapter to finish.				
25. His eyes were *literally* standing out of his head.				
26. They invited my friends and *myself*.				
27. What are the chances of *them* being found out?				
28. Intoxication is *when* the brain is affected by certain stimulants.				
29. Their success, his attitude *inferred*, was due to his own efforts.				
30. He refused *to even think* of it.				
31. They would accept this if it *was* offered.				
32. He did it *quicker* than he had ever done it before.				
33. He did not actually dislike football; he was just *disinterested*.				
34. Reference will be made to the *historic* development of mathematics.				
35. Neither author nor publisher *are* subject to censorship.				

Appendix

	Informal		Formal	
	Speech	Writing	Speech	Writing
36. One rarely likes to do as *he* is told.				
37. Roller-skating is very different *to* ice-skating.				
38. *These sort of plays* need first-class acting.				
39. You will learn that *at university*.				
40. *Pulling the trigger*, the gun went off unexpectedly.				
41. He could write *as well or better than* most people.				
42. She told Charles and *I* the whole story.				
43. It was *us* who had been singing.				
44. Nowadays Sunday is not observed *like* it used to be.				
45. He told me the story and I *implied* a great deal from it.				
46. They bought some tomatoes *off* a barrow-boy.				
47. It looked *like* it would rain.				
48. I *will* be twenty-one tomorrow.				
49. Everyone has *their* off-days.				
50. They will *loan* you the glasses.				
51. He jumped *onto* the roof of the shed.				
52. *Who* was he looking for?				
53. That's a dangerous curve; you'd better go *slow*.				
54. In spite of the delay, everything was *alright*.				
55. Between you and *I*, she drinks heavily.				

(Originally published in W. H. Mittins, Mary Salu, Mary Edminson, and Sheila Coyne, *Attitudes to English Usage*. London: Oxford University Press, 1970.)

Current Usage in Grammar
(as ranked by linguists)

Sterling A. Leonard

Established Usages
1. *A Tale of Two Cities* is *an* historical novel.
2. It was *I* that broke the vase, father.
3. Why *pursue* a vain hope?
4. *One* rarely enjoys *one's* luncheon when *one* is tired.
5. The invalid was able *partially to raise* his body.
6. It *behooves* them to take action at once.
7. I *had rather* go at once.
8. *In this connection,* I should add ...
9. This is a man ... I used to know. (Omitted relative.)
10. You *had better* stop that foolishness.
11. Each person should of course bear *his or her* share of the expense.
12. Galileo discovered that the earth *moved.*
13. This hat is *not so* large as mine.
14. My position in the company was satisfactory from every *point of view.*
15. He toils *to the end that* he may amass wealth.
16. *In the case* of students who elect an extra subject, an additional fee is charged.
17. The defendant's case was *hurt* by this admission.
18. *I for one* hope he will be there.
19. This is the chapter *whose* contents cause most discussion.
20. *Under these circumstances* I will concede the point.
21. I have no prejudices, and *that* is the cause of my unpopularity.
22. You may ask *whomsoever* you please.
23. The honest person is to be *applauded.*
24. He stood *in front of* the class to speak.
25. *This much* is certain.
26. He did not do *as* well *as* we expected.
27. We *got home* at three o'clock.
28. He has no fear; nothing can *confuse* him.
29. There is a large *works* near the bridge.
30. *As regards the League,* let me say ...
31. "You just had a telephone call." "Did *they* leave any message?"
32. I was attacked by one of *those* huge police dogs.
33. The women were *all dressed up.*
34. This was the *reason why* he went home.
35. This book is valueless, that one has more to recommend it. (Comma splice.)
36. Take two *cups* of flour.
37. *None* of them *are* here.

Appendix

38. I *drove* the car around the block.
39. He doesn't do it *the way* I do.
40. The New York climate is *healthiest* in fall.
41. I felt I could walk no *further.*
42. One is not *fit* to vote at the age of eighteen.
43. Our catch was *pretty* good.
44. We have made some progress *along these lines.*
45. The catcher stands *back of* the home plate.
46. My colleagues and I *shall* be glad to help you.
47. I went immediately into the banquet room, *which* was, I found later, a technical error.
48. That will be *all right,* you may be sure.
49. We will *try and get* it.
50. We cannot discover *from whence* this rumor emanates.
51. I can hardly *stand* him.
52. Jane *was home* all last week.
53. *I'd like* to make a correction.
54. I've absolutely *got* to go.
55. We can expect the commission *to at least protect* our interests.
56. That's a dangerous curve; you'd better go *slow.*
57. There are some *nice* people here.
58. *Will* you be at the Browns' this evening?
59. Have you *fixed* the fire for the night?
60. I don't know *if* I can.
61. *In hopes of* seeing you, I asked . . .
62. *It* says in the book that . . .
63. If it *wasn't* for football, school life would be dull.
64. His attack on my motives made me *peevish.*
65. We *taxied* to the station to catch the train.
66. We *only* had one left.
67. My *viewpoint* on this is that we ought to make concessions.
68. Factories were *mostly* closed on election day.
69. He moves mighty *quick* on a tennis court.
70. He stopped to *price* some flowers.
71. He worked with much *snap.*
72. This room is *awfully* cold.
73. It is *me.*
74. *Who* are you looking for?
75. A treaty was concluded *between the four powers.*
76. *You* had to have property to vote, in the eighteenth century.
77. The kind of apples you mean *are* large and sour.
78. I have a *heap* of work to do.
79. I *felt badly* about his death.

80. The real *reason* he failed *was because* he tried to do too much.
81. Invite *whoever* you like to the party.
82. Drive *slow* down that hill!
83. Harry was a little shaver about *this* tall.
84. I didn't speak to my uncle by long distance; I couldn't *get through*.
85. *They* had numerous strikes in England.
86. I will go, *providing* you keep away.
87. I have *got* my own opinion on that.
88. He made a *date* for next week.
89. My father walked very *slow* down the street.
90. There *was* a bed, a dresser, and two chairs in the room.
91. They invited my friends and *myself*.
92. It is now *plain and evident* why he left.
93. I wish I *was* wonderful.
94. I've no doubt *but what* he will come.
95. What was the reason for *Bennett making* that disturbance?
96. *Can* I be excused from this class?
97. Haven't you *got through* yet?
98. *Everyone* was here, but *they* all went home early.
99. He *loaned* me his skates.
100. My *folks* sent me a check.
101. He came *around* four o'clock.
102. If it had been *us,* we would admit it.
103. They went *way* around by the orchard road.
104. The banker *loaned* me $200 at 6%.
105. *Pikes* Peak is in Colorado.
106. The sailors *laid* out along the yards.
107. Is your insurance sufficient *coverage* for your house?

Disputable Usages

108. That clock must be *fixed*.
109. My contention has been *proven* many times.
110. Sam, who was then in town, was with me *the three or four first* days.
111. *One* rarely likes to do as *he* is told.
112. He never works *evenings* or *Sundays*.
113. They have *gotten* a new car this year.
114. The Rock Island *depot* burned down last night.
115. Sitting *in back of* John, he said, "Now guess what I have."
116. I took it to be *they*.
117. I *guess* I'll go to lunch.
118. He went *right* home and told his father.
119. He could write *as well* or *better than I*.
120. I *expect* he knows his subject.

Appendix

121. I *can't seem* to get this problem right.
122. I was pretty *mad* about it.
123. *Either* of these *three* roads is good.
124. You are older than *me*.
125. What are the chances of *them* being found out?
126. There is *a* big *woods* behind the house.
127. I know it to be *he*.
128. Do you *wish* for some ice cream?
129. Intoxication is *when* the brain is affected by certain stimulants.
130. *Neither* of your reasons *are* really valid.
131. He *dove* off the pier.
132. Trollope's novels have already begun to *date*.
133. Will you go? *Sure*.
134. He is *kind of silly*, I think.
135. I *will probably* come a little late.
136. That was the reason for *me leaving* school.
137. They *eat* (et) dinner at twelve o'clock.
138. I'll swear that was *him*.
139. Well, that's *going some*.
140. *Leave* me alone, or else get out.
141. Of two disputants, the *warmest* is generally in the wrong.
142. It was *good and cold* when I came in.
143. We haven't *but* a few left.
144. In the collision with a Packard, our car naturally got the *worse* of it.
145. I wouldn't have said that if I had thought it *would have* shocked her.
146. *Yourself* and your guests are invited.
147. The man was *very amused*.
148. Such *naif* actions seem to me absurd.
149. It seems to be *them*.
150. Everybody bought *their* own ticket.
151. *Say*, do you know who that is?
152. I suppose that's *him*.
153. I *can't help but* eat it.
154. *Aren't* ('nt or rnt) I right?
155. There is a row of beds with a curtain *between each bed*.
156. If I asked him, he would *likely* refuse.
157. John didn't do so *bad* this time.
158. Cities and villages are being stripped of all they contain *not only*, but often of their very inhabitants.
159. *Everybody's else* affairs are his concern.
160. It *don't* make any difference what you think.
161. I read in the paper *where* a plane was lost.
162. That boy's mischievous behavior *aggravates* me.

163. That stock market collapse left me *busted*.
164. Neither author nor publisher *are* subject to censorship.
165. Yes, our plan worked just *fine*.
166. The fire captain with his loyal men *were* cheered.
167. Don't get *these* kind of gloves.
168. The British look at this differently *than* we do.
169. *Most* anybody can do that.
170. It is *liable* to snow tonight.
171. They went in *search for* the missing child.
172. I suppose I'm wrong, *ain't* I?
173. John was *raised* by his aunt.
174. Martha *don't* sew as well as she used to.
175. He *most* always does what his wife tells him.
176. It *sure* was good to see Uncle Charles.
177. My experience on the farm helped me *some*, of course.
178. It's *real* cold today.
179. His presence was valueless *not only*, but a hindrance as well.
180. We don't often see sunsets *like* they have in the tropics.
181. I am older than *him*.
182. She leaped off *of* the moving car.
183. She *sung* very well.
184. It is only a little *ways* farther.
185. It looked *like* they meant business.
186. Do it *like* he tells you.
187. The child was weak, *due to* improper feeding.

Uncultivated or Illiterate Usages

188. John *had awoken* much earlier than usual.
189. I have*n't hardly* any money.
190. The engine was hitting *good* this morning.
191. The dessert was made with *whip* cream.
192. Now just *where* are we *at*?
193. The kitten mews whenever it *wants in*.
194. A woman *whom* I know was my friend spoke next.
195. He *drunk* too much ice water.
196. *Reverend Jones* will preach.
197. All came except *she*.
198. The *party* who wrote that was a scholar.
199. My Uncle John, *he* told me a story.
200. He *begun* to make excuses.
201. I *calculate* to go soon.
202. This is *all the further* I can read.
203. That *ain't* so.

Appendix

204. The *data is* often inaccurate.
205. He looked at me and *says* ...
206. I must go and *lay* down.
207. *Ain't* that just like a man?
208. Both leaves of the drawbridge *raise* at once.
209. The people *which* were here have all gone.
210. I *have drank* all my milk.
211. *That there* rooster is a fighter.
212. The old poodle was *to no sense* agreeable.
213. One of my brothers *were* helping me.
214. I enjoy wandering *among* a library.
215. A light *complected* girl passed.
216. I want *for you to come* at once.
217. He won't *leave* me come in.
218. There was *a* orange in the dish.
219. It was dark when he *come* in.
220. You *was* mistaken about that, John.
221. I wish he *hadn't of* come.
222. *Hadn't* you *ought* to ask your mother?
223. My cold *wa'nt* any better next day.
224. If John *had of* come, I needn't have.
225. I had hardly *laid* down again when the phone rang.
226. He did *noble*.
227. Somebody *run* past just as I opened the door.
228. Just *set* down and rest awhile.
229. The neighbors took turns *setting* up with him.
230. They *swang* their partners in the reel.

(Originally published in Albert H. Marckwardt and Fred G. Walcott, *Facts About Current English Usage*. New York: Appleton-Century, 1938.)

Quinn's Quiz

Forget about Theodore Bernstein, forget about the Wonderful English Teacher. Take this simple test, and compare your own ideas of correct grammar and diction with the great writers and experts of the past.

1. All debts are cleared between you and (I, me)
   Shakespeare, *Merchant of Venice*, III, ii, 321.
2. Brain Worm has been with my cousin Edward and (I, me) all this day.
   Jonson, *Every Man in His Humor*, V, iii.
3. The Space (between, among) the three points . . . the treaty (between, among) the three powers.
   Oxford English Dictionary.
4. If a person is born of a gloomy temper (they, he, he or she) cannot help it.
   Chesterfield, *Letters*, IV, ccclv, 170.
5. Nobody does anything well that (they, he, he or she) cannot help doing.
   Ruskin, *Crown of Wild Olives*, No. 38.
6. (There's, There're) two of you.
   Shakespeare, *2 Henry VI*, III, ii, 303.
7. That last foul thing Thou ever (author'dst, wrote).
   Chapman, *Iliad*, I, 231.
8. Ilka ain to be liable for their ain (input, contribution).
   Scott, *Heart of the Midlothian*, xii.
9. He talks (like, as) Brunswick did.
   Southey, *Letters*, I, 12.
10. Unfortunately, few have observed (like, as) you have done.
    Darwin, *Life and Letters*, III, 58.
11. Lord Delaware is considerably younger than (me, I).
    Byron, *Letters*, 2 Nov. 1804.
12. Typhus fever (decimated, killed a large number in) the school periodically.
    Charlotte Bronte, Letter, in Mrs. Gaskell's *Life*, 276.
13. All these three, like, went together. (or "All these three went together.")
    Richardson, *Pamela*, I, 238.
14. Consider first, that Great and Bright (infers, implies) no excellence.
    Milton, *Paradise Lost*, VIII, 91.
15. The Whitish gleam was . . . conferred by the (enormity, enormousness) of their remotion.
    De Quincey, *The System of the Heavens*, III, 183.
16. (These, This) kind of knaves I know.
    Shakespeare, *King Lear*, II, ii, 107.
17. The consuls . . . had been elected from very different merits (than, from) those of skill in war.
    Goldsmith, *Roman History*, I, 105.
18. (Who, Whom) are you speaking of?
    Hardy, *Far from the Madding Crowd*, 170.

Appendix

19. (Who, Whom) do you think?
    Idiomatic.
20. The Lord knows (who, whom)!
    Idiomatic.

And a special bonus, for the extra careful user of language; fill in the blank:

21. A (the prefix meaning not or without) should be prefixed only to Greek stems . . . "Amoral," being literary, is inexcusable. _____ should be used instead.
    H. W. Fowler, *Modern English Usage*, page 1.

1. I.	11. me
2. I	12. decimate
3. between	13. like (belike)
4. they	14. infers
5. they	15. enormity
6. there's	16. these kind
7. author'dst	17. different than
8. input	18. who
9. like	19. who
10. like	20. who

21. This question is only included to show where the principles of logic and etymology applied to language can lead. Fowler, who thought the word paleolithic a barbarism, insists that the proper word should be *nonmoral.* Which is a nice word. Fowler must have had fun using it. But it doesn't mean *amoral* to me. Does it to anyone?

(Originally published in Jim Quinn's "Plain English," *Washington Post Magazine* (December 11, 1977), pp. 14-16, 34-36.)

Language Inquiry

Ellen A. Frogner

Part I

Directions

Check the column that most nearly represents your response to each of the statements that follow. Wherever the question concerns usage, consider the statement in relation to American English unless otherwise specified.
   1 = Agree—definite agreement (complete or nearly so)
   2 = Moderately agree—agreement with reservations
   3 = No opinion—no opinion either way and therefore the response might be described as neutral
   4 = Disagree—definite disagreement (complete or nearly so)
Be sure to circle only one of the choices for each statement.

Statements

1. Teachers should insist on formal English in the classroom, both in speaking and writing. (1 2 3 4)
2. The signs saying *Drive Slow* should be corrected to read *Drive Slowly*. (1 2 3 4)
3. A native speaker of English has an operational knowledge of his language without instruction in it. (1 2 3 4)
4. Linguists now know the characteristics that the English language should have. (1 2 3 4)
5. A college student made the following comment to his friend: *If the time was longer between quarters, I'd go down to Florida or somewhere.* He should have used *were* instead of *was* in the *if* clause. (1 2 3 4)
6. Verbless sentences are frequently effective in descriptive writing. (1 2 3 4)
7. The speakers of Chinese and English use some of the same methods to signal meaning. (1 2 3 4)
8. An outline written according to a standard form is a prerequisite to the successful writing of an essay. (1 2 3 4)
9. One looks in vain for order in English spelling. (1 2 3 4)
10. The illogical sequence in a sentence like *She drove back and forth every day* is confusing even to many native users of English. (1 2 3 4)
11. People who speak differently from the majority follow some pattern of regularity in the English language. (1 2 3 4)
12. It is only within the last ten years that there has been any questioning of the classifications found in traditional grammar. (1 2 3 4)
13. A student who thinks independently would be skeptical about the common textbook definition *A noun is a word that names*. (1 2 3 4)
14. Even though *It's me* is accepted in informal English, the expression *It is I* is really right. (1 2 3 4)

Appendix 91

15. The use of words like *terrific* and *O.K.* for approval is sometimes in good taste. (1 2 3 4)
16. Meanings of words are based on consent (acceptance) within a speech community. (1 2 3 4)
17. A redundant expression cannot be standard usage. (1 2 3 4)
18. The structure of German is more like that of English than the structure of Latin is. (1 2 3 4)
19. The words *linguistics* and *grammar* are synonyms. (1 2 3 4)
20. Since *silly* once had the more elevated meaning of *happy*, it has degenerated as a word. (1 2 3 4)
21. Standard English allows for no choices in language forms. (1 2 3 4)
22. The child's development in the use of language during the preschool years provides clues for methods to be used in the English classroom. (1 2 3 4)
23. As soon as we take present-day usage for a guide in determining what is acceptable English, we break down all standards. (1 2 3 4)
24. Linguists look upon their work as that of controlling the language, of keeping it within bounds. (1 2 3 4)
25. If twentieth-century standards in language were higher, there would be no instances of divided usage in pronunciation. (1 2 3 4)
26. Adherence to the conventions of spelling can easily be overestimated as a characteristic of a good composition. (1 2 3 4)
27. The usual composition textbook is a sound guide to facts about English usage. (1 2 3 4)
28. The use of word order as a way to show meaning has developed in English grammar mainly since Shakespeare's time. (1 2 3 4)
29. The English language is more a product of historical accident than it is of the efforts of the grammarians, lexicographers, or critics who have wanted to shape it. (1 2 3 4)
30. Students should be taught that **they** must place a comma after every introductory clause or phrase **coming** before the subject of a sentence. (1 2 3 4)
31. To most people *He's not going nowhere* means that the person spoken about is going somewhere. (1 2 3 4)
32. The English language is limited mainly to *shall* and *will* for expressing future time. (1 2 3 4)
33. Modern dictionary editors base definitions on context. (1 2 3 4)
34. The spelling *aesthetic* should be used because it reflects the origin of the word better than does the spelling *esthetic*. (1 2 3 4)
35. Good writing is recorded speaking. (1 2 3 4)
36. Students should be discouraged from using the inductive method in the development of an essay. (1 2 3 4)
37. What happened in the English language in the past has little relationship to what is happening now. (1 2 3 4)
38. Drill in conjugating English verbs is of little consequence to the native speaker. (1 2 3 4)

39. In giving a talk on tennis, a high school student in southern Illinois used the pronunciation *tinnis*. He was told that regional pronunciations would not be accepted in the English class. More teachers should use the same method. (1 2 3 4)
40. Whoever learns a language learns an alphabet. (1 2 3 4)
41. Usage, not redundancy, makes *this here* a nonstandard (substandard) expression in English. (1 2 3 4)
42. Because of the preposition at the end, the following sentence is not accepted as standard English: *The young man now had something to work for.* (1 2 3 4)
43. A drama group in the Middle West used the spelling *theater* in the name of their organization. They should have used *theatre* because it is a better spelling. (1 2 3 4)
44. The more rules of language an individual can state, the better speaker or writer he will be. (1 2 3 4)
45. Since the *k* in *knowledge* is not pronounced, we should promote reform in spelling by omitting this letter in our own writing. (1 2 3 4)
46. Today we make constant use of words derived from the native stock brought to England from the continent at the beginning of the Old English period. (1 2 3 4)
47. In English classes, a study of pronouns in the objective case should be preceded by a study of nouns in the objective case. (1 2 3 4)
48. A college senior made the statement: "I am going to student-teach next quarter." The expression *to student-teach* represents a process made use of mainly in college campus English. (1 2 3 4)
49. Standards in English are relative, not absolute. (1 2 3 4)
50. English that is free of idiom is English well used. (1 2 3 4)
51. It is normal for people to have a strong attachment for the language they use. (1 2 3 4)
52. The bigger the words used, the more effective the expression. (1 2 3 4)
53. The rule *Two or more singular subjects connected by "and" require a plural verb* does not always apply in standard English. (1 2 3 4)
54. Because there is already so little grammatical inflection left in English, teachers should support the use of the inflected form rather than the phrase to state the genitive (possessive). The expression *the course's value* would then be preferable to *the value of the course*. (1 2 3 4)
55. Twentieth-century standards of scholarship in dictionary compiling and editing are low as compared with those of the eighteenth century. (1 2 3 4)
56. It is up to English teachers to see that our language does not change. (1 2 3 4)
57. To say that an expression is colloquial is to say that it is not entirely acceptable. (1 2 3 4)
58. Every speaker of English uses at least one dialect, often more than one. (1 2 3 4)

Appendix 93

59. Written English is the foundation on which spoken English rests. (1 2 3 4)
60. The following sentence represents standard English usage: *A financial arrangement was worked out between the chorus, band, and orchestra.* (1 2 3 4)
61. Standard American English is a group of dialects within American English. (1 2 3 4)
62. A study of English grammar should be concerned with relationships between sentences as well as within sentences. (1 2 3 4)
63. The title "It Makes a Difference" needs to be re-stated because the pronoun has no antecedent. (1 2 3 4)
64. Change in language is normal, but so also is continuity. (1 2 3 4)
65. Grammatical rules stated in textbooks and handbooks determine what is accepted English and what is not accepted. (1 2 3 4)
66. Splitting the infinitive may sometimes enable the writer to express his ideas with greater clarity and force than otherwise. (1 2 3 4)
67. In teaching students how to write a letter of application, a teacher said, "Don't talk down to the person who will read your letter. Don't, then, use many one-syllable words." This was sound advice. (1 2 3 4)
68. Students in American high schools should be informed that the pronunciation *prō-cess* is preferable to *prŏ-cess*. (1 2 3 4)
69. A person should be criticized for the use of *if* instead of *whether* in a sentence like *I'll see if there is a tape recorder in the room.* (1 2 3 4)
70. Punctuation may conform to the customary rules and yet be stylistically poor. (1 2 3 4)
71. A teacher told his students that Latin is a better language than English. He was accurate in his statement. (1 2 3 4)
72. An individual may acquire an intuitive mastery of the form and order of English. (1 2 3 4)
73. Current activity in the area of grammatical theory and method reflects a confidence that the right answers have now been found. (1 2 3 4)
74. For most people, the patterns of the native language are largely established during the preschool years. (1 2 3 4)
75. In directing a Shakespearean play, a college dramatics coach in the Kentucky foothills insisted that the students substitute twentieth-century platform English pronunciation for their regional dialect forms. He should be complimented for taking this stand. (1 2 3 4)
76. Contractions are inappropriate in any form of written English. (1 2 3 4)
77. The following sentence is being analyzed: *John will look up the current value of the English pound.* It seems sensible to consider *will look up* as the verb; however it is not correct to do so, since *up* has to be either an adverb or a preposition. (1 2 3 4)
78. Comma-splice sentences (independent clauses or main statements with just a comma between) have justifiable uses. (1 2 3 4)
79. We should have an American Academy to regulate our language. (1 2 3 4)

80. A child who asks permission by saying *Can I go too?* should not have his English corrected by being told to say *May I go too?* (1 2 3 4)
81. Proficiency in speaking depends on proficiency in writing. (1 2 3 4)
82. The pronunciation used in the Middle West is not as good as that used in the East. (1 2 3 4)
83. The forms used in nonstandard English are a degeneration of the forms used in standard English. (1 2 3 4)
84. Language that aims to arouse emotion should be distrusted *per se*. (1 2 3 4)
85. Statements (a) and (b) are at different levels of abstraction; (a) I gave her the book this morning. (b) *Her* is the indirect object, and *book* is the direct object. (1 2 3 4)
86. Metaphors are used mainly in literary English. (1 2 3 4)
87. There is more than one variety of accepted English usage. (1 2 3 4)
88. Any essays except the most informal must be written from the third person objective point of view. (1 2 3 4)
89. Finding the elements of which a sentence is composed—primary, secondary, and tertiary—is a method that has appeared within the last decade. (1 2 3 4)
90. A person cannot use sentences until he can describe (talk about) subjects and predicates. (1 2 3 4)
91. The word *number* is singular in form but may be either singular or plural in thought. (1 2 3 4)
92. A teacher should drill strenuously on *Whom do you mean* as the correct form. (1 2 3 4)
93. In using language, we are abstracting experience. (1 2 3 4)
94. A description of a grammatical system must not be identified as being the system itself. (1 2 3 4)
95. A truly cultivated person will pronounce the word *either* as *ī-ther* (not *ē-ther*). (1 2 3 4)
96. In writing a summary of a story, a student has just finished explaining what the life of the main character has been like. The student then goes on: "But now there is nothing for Larry to look forward to except a nice-paying office job and invitations to the right parties." The writer was wrong in beginning a sentence with *but*. (1 2 3 4)
97. The following sentence is quoted from a book review written in an English class: "Paula doesn't want Smithy to join the crowd of compromisers and money makers." The sentence should be corrected for the use of a contraction. (1 2 3 4)
98. Change in language is inevitable. (1 2 3 4)
99. The etymology of a word determines whether or not it is accepted as standard English. (1 2 3 4)
100. The process of learning a language differs from the process of learning historical facts. (1 2 3 4)

(Originally published in Ellen A. Frogner's *Using the Language Inquiry as a Teaching Device*. Washington, D.C.: Bureau of Research, Office of Education, U.S. Department of Health, Education and Welfare, 1969.)

Appendix

Language Attitudes and Information Study

by Susan H. Houston

For each sentence check A if you agree with the sentence and D if you disagree with it.

__A __D 1. It would be good to have an international language.
__A __D 2. All languages are similar in some important ways.
__A __D 3. English is more closely related to German than to French.
__A __D 4. Languages in Africa, and American Indian languages, are often primitive and simple in structure.
__A __D 5. You can frequently tell if someone is an American, a Frenchman, an Italian, etc., just by the way he gestures when talking.
__A __D 6. The pronunciation of educated Blacks usually cannot be distinguished from that of educated Whites.
__A __D 7. It is better for a language (such as English) to make up new words when they are needed than to borrow words from other languages.
__A __D 8. Adults have difficulty learning foreign languages because their vocal mechanisms become frozen into the positions of their native language.
__A __D 9. Few people from lower-class homes can speak correct English without slang.
__A __D 10. Children who are three or four years old can learn two languages at a time without confusion.
__A __D 11. Many different kinds of animals (for instance birds, wolves, monkeys) have languages of their own similar in structure, grammar, and function to human languages.
__A __D 12. If your pronunciation of a word is different from the one the dictionary gives, this may be because the dictionary fails to reflect modern popular usage.
__A __D 13. The only effective way to teach American Indian children the English language is to prevent them from speaking their native language while in school.
__A __D 14. Having learned Latin will not necessarily help you in learning another language.
__A __D 15. Black speech is not Black persons' main handicap in getting good jobs or achieving social acceptance.
__A __D 16. Someone can learn how to speak correctly without ever studying grammar in school.
__A __D 17. The words *piece* and *peace* are spelled differently because they are pronounced a little differently.
__A __D 18. The best way to teach foreign languages is to start when children first come to school.
__A __D 19. Computers have not been successful in translating books or articles from Russian to English.

__A __D 20. One of the main problems of Spanish-Americans trying to learn English is that they tend to run their words together instead of pronouncing each word distinctly.

__A __D 21. People from the South and West should try to talk like people from the Midwest and the East, instead of with an accent.

__A __D 22. Many stutterers can be helped if someone will remind them frequently to speak more slowly.

__A __D 23. Children who are punished for talking in adult company will nevertheless be able to learn language without difficulty.

__A __D 24. Most bilinguals (people who grow up learning two languages) cannot speak either language really well, and so are often not as intelligent as people who speak only one language.

__A __D 25. Even as children, Americans are less gifted at learning foreign languages than people in other countries.

__A __D 26. The language of Blacks in America is very similar to that of Whites, and therefore Black children do not need to be taught English as though it were a foreign language.

__A __D 27. If a German baby is raised by an American family in the United States, he will speak English without any trace of a German accent.

__A __D 28. Some languages are so primitive that they cannot express every concept they need, so that their speakers are forced to fill in with grunts and gestures.

__A __D 29. To learn a foreign language, you need only have a good complete dictionary.

__A __D 30. Some African languages can be "spoken" by drum signals.

__A __D 31. Most Blacks speak English poorly because it is too complex a language for them to master fully.

__A __D 32. Children who speak a foreign language at home with their parents may still learn to speak English without a foreign accent.

__A __D 33. English is no easier to learn than other languages and so would have no particular advantage as an international language.

__A __D 34. Modern popular songs, especially rock songs, reflect the decay of the English language.

__A __D 35. No dog, cat or other house pet can understand everything that is said to it.

__A __D 36. The speech of Blacks sounds different from that of Whites because Black speech has a higher percent of slang in it.

__A __D 37. Forcing a left-handed child to become right-handed will not make him stutter.

__A __D 38. English spelling bears almost no relationship to the spoken language and so should be simplified.

__A __D 39. In some languages a noun may not be best defined as "the name of a person, place, or thing."

Appendix 97

__A __D 40. A British or New York accent is generally a sign of snobbishness or arrogance.

__A __D 41. Disadvantaged or culturally deprived children usually do not speak English well enough to succeed at school or to form abstract thoughts.

__A __D 42. Foreigners who live for many years in the United States without learning English are showing that they do not really like this country.

__A __D 43. Both Blacks and Whites use slang for the same reasons: sometimes for fun, and sometimes to prevent others from understanding what they are saying.

__A __D 44. Most well-educated people usually speak in complete sentences.

__A __D 45. The English language has hardly changed at all, except perhaps for spelling, since it began.

__A __D 46. Carrying on conversations with infants who have not yet begun to speak, and talking to them a lot, often confuses them and is bad for their language development.

__A __D 47. Learning a foreign language, especially Latin, improves and disciplines the mind.

__A __D 48. American children can learn to speak English well without ever studying it in school.

__A __D 49. The fact that some Black people's lips are shaped somewhat differently from those of White people has no effect upon differences between the sounds of Black and White speech.

__A __D 50. Adults can rarely learn to speak a foreign language like native speakers.

__A __D 51. People who put long pauses between their words when they speak are trying to hide some of their true thoughts.

__A __D 52. Some animals occasionally communicate by mental telepathy.

__A __D 53. There are many unwritten languages in the world.

__A __D 54. American Indians have great difficulty learning English because their own language and culture are so much less complicated.

__A __D 55. Black children should be taught Standard English (for instance, the kind spoken on the radio or TV) instead of being allowed to go on speaking Black English.

__A __D 56. The reason that many immigrants cannot seem to lose their foreign accents is that their verbal abilities are not equal to those of most Americans.

__A __D 57. Children's language may be permanently harmed if they read comic books or cheap popular novels.

__A __D 58. Parents usually do not need to seek help for children who are slow in learning to talk or who mispronounce many words, since children often behave in these ways just to gain attention and will outgrow such behavior if it is ignored.

___A ___D 59. Studying grammar in school is of great practical value.

___A ___D 60. It takes children no longer to learn to speak languages such as Russian or Chinese than it takes them to learn English.

___A ___D 61. Everyone should study a foreign language, at least for a short while.

___A ___D 62. The main reason Blacks sometimes do not pronounce all the sounds in a word is that they lack the initiative or drive to learn correct English.

___A ___D 63. Children are able to begin learning to read when they are very young, even as young as two or three, and this will benefit their language development.

___A ___D 64. People who say "uh" or "mm" a lot are probably nervous or upset.

___A ___D 65. It is better to learn a foreign language from someone who is a native speaker of the language (that is, grew up in the country where it is spoken and spoke the language all his life) than from an American.

___A ___D 66. The language of Black children shows that they have such important concepts as past tense, plural, future, and how to ask questions properly.

___A ___D 67. People who prefer using slang may be able to use correct English equally as well when the occasion demands it.

___A ___D 68. An adult foreigner learning English, or an adult American learning a foreign language, will probably always have a foreign accent in the new language unless he spends many years in the country where it is spoken.

___A ___D 69. The words *often* and *coffin* really rhyme, even though *often* has a "t" in it.

___A ___D 70. Porpoises (dolphins) can understand human speech.

___A ___D 71. All Americans should learn general standard English in school, instead of speaking some dialect of English.

___A ___D 72. If a Black baby is raised by a White family in a White neighborhood, his speech will nevertheless sound very different from the speech of Whites.

___A ___D 73. It is a good practice to try to write the way you speak.

___A ___D 74. It is not essential for Americans to learn foreign languages, since by now most people in other countries have learned to speak and understand English.

___A ___D 75. Babies have their own language before they learn to speak a regular language, and they can all communicate with each other.

___A ___D 76. English does not come from Latin.

___A ___D 77. It is possible for a child to learn language and understand it perfectly even though he never seems to talk at all.

Appendix 99

__A __D 78. The more highly organized and civilized a culture is, the more likely it is to have simplified its language to make it more efficient.

__A __D 79. Spanish-Americans have difficulty learning English because they speak their own language so rapidly.

__A __D 80. The rhythm of Black language reflects Black people's natural love of and ability in music.

__A __D 81. If a Chinese baby is raised by an American family, he will still tend to speak Chinese.

__A __D 82. School integration has not been a bad influence on the language of White middle-class children in America.

__A __D 83. The Chinese have good reasons which are not political for refusing to adopt the English alphabet in writing their language.

__A __D 84. In some languages, men and women speak so differently that they cannot understand each other or communicate at all.

__A __D 85. It is incorrect or substandard English to pronounce the word *says* as though it were written "sez."

__A __D 86. If Blacks would pronounce their words more clearly, they would have far less difficulty getting along with Whites.

__A __D 87. The speech of people in isolated mountain areas of America is actually the English of Shakespeare's time.

__A __D 88. Adults whose language has been impaired through brain injury have much more difficulty relearning language than young children with similar injuries.

__A __D 89. People who speak with a foreign accent can never be considered truly American.

__A __D 90. Babies can usually understand speech even before they can speak themselves.

__A __D 91. The kind of English spoken by Black children does not in itself handicap them in learning to read.

__A __D 92. People who use a great many long words when talking are generally trying to show everyone how intelligent they think they are.

__A __D 93. There is no evidence that television has a bad effect on children's language.

__A __D 94. The harsh, guttural sounds of German provide an insight into the German character.

__A __D 95. Children do not need formal instruction in foreign languages or in English, since they learn to speak just by listening to other people talking.

__A __D 96. Black language and White language are both about equally creative and expressive.

__A __D 97. A large number of American children and adults can hardly read at all.
__A __D 98. Children who speak a foreign language at home and English at school become confused and do poorly at their studies.
__A __D 99. Deaf children should not be permitted to learn a sign language, since this prevents their thoughts from developing fully and impairs abstract communication.
__A __D 100. Children who start to speak somewhat late may be just as intelligent as those who start to speak earlier.
__A __D 101. American children learn English, French children learn French, and so on, because they are born with a tendency to learn their own particular language.
__A __D 102. Many parrots and parakeets can speak and understand English, and carry on conversations.
__A __D 103. Any foreigner who lives more than ten years in the United States without learning English should be sent back to his native country.
__A __D 104. Most Black children can easily understand the language of White teachers in school.
__A __D 105. Since all American Indians speak closely related languages, they can always communicate with each other.
__A __D 106. The Eskimo language has hundreds of different words for "snow."
__A __D 107. More schools should have bilingual education programs for Spanish-speaking children.
__A __D 108. Most people with heavy Southern accents are relatively uneducated and often quite prejudiced.
__A __D 109. Some chimpanzees (apes) have been taught sign language or other forms of communication which they have learned with the same ease and fluency as a human child does.
__A __D 110. A child who seems unable to learn to read is probably either somewhat retarded or in need of firmer discipline.
__A __D 111. A hearing child who is raised by deaf parents will usually pick up spoken language easily from his friends and teachers.
__A __D 112. A child who is spoiled by his parents and has all his needs met without having to ask for things will probably not learn language until late in his development.
__A __D 113. A Japanese baby raised by an American family in the United States will learn English, but somewhat more slowly than an American infant would.
__A __D 114. Language delay in children is most often caused by factors other than mental retardation.
__A __D 115. Working-class and uneducated persons speak differently in different social settings, whereas the educated middle-class person tends to speak in about the same way all the time.

Appendix 101

__A __D 116. Very few utterances made by children are imitations of sentences they have heard adults speak.

__A __D 117. Minority dialects in America generally show a lack of logic and poor organization of thoughts on the part of their speakers, as demonstrated by their frequent grammatical errors.

__A __D 118. The sign language used by many deaf children and adults has no grammar, and is just a series of gestures standing for concrete objects.

__A __D 119. Children who stutter or have reading difficulties need to be taught better coordination, through such methods as instruction in crawling and walking, and use of the right hand in eating.

__A __D 120. A child with a language or hearing problem can benefit from language therapy even before he is of school age.

(Originally published in *English Journal* 67 (March 1978): 33-38.)

Taylor's Language Attitude Scale

Circle a number indicating your opinion for each statement: 1 = strong disagreement, 2 = mild disagreement, 3 = mild agreement, 4 = strong agreement, 5 = no opinion.

1 2 3 4 5   The scholastic level of a school will fall if teachers allow Black English to be spoken.
1 2 3 4 5   Black English is a misuse of Standard English.
1 2 3 4 5   Attempts to eliminate Black English in school result in a situation which can be psychologically damaging to black children.
1 2 3 4 5   Continued usage of a nonstandard dialect of English would accomplish nothing worthwhile for society.
1 2 3 4 5   Black English sounds as good as Standard English.
1 2 3 4 5   Teachers should allow black students to use Black English in the classroom.
1 2 3 4 5   Black English should be discouraged.
1 2 3 4 5   Black English must be accepted if pride is to develop among black people.
1 2 3 4 5   Black English is an inferior language system.
1 2 3 4 5   Black English is cool.
1 2 3 4 5   Black English should be considered a bad influence on American culture and civilization.
1 2 3 4 5   Black English sounds sloppy.
1 2 3 4 5   If use of Black English were encouraged, speakers of Black English would be more motivated to achieve academically.
1 2 3 4 5   Black English is a clear, thoughtful, and expressive language.
1 2 3 4 5   Black English has a faulty grammar system.
1 2 3 4 5   When teachers reject the native language of a student, they do him great harm.
1 2 3 4 5   A teacher should correct a student's use of Nonstandard English.
1 2 3 4 5   In a predominantly black school, Black English as well as Standard English should be taught.
1 2 3 4 5   Widespread acceptance of Black English is imperative.
1 2 3 4 5   The sooner we eliminate nonstandard dialects of English, the better.
1 2 3 4 5   Acceptance of nonstandard dialects of English by teachers will lead to a lowering of standards in schools.
1 2 3 4 5   Nonstandard English should be accepted socially.
1 2 3 4 5   Nonstandard English is as effective for communication as is Standard English.

Appendix

1 2 3 4 5 One of the goals of the American school system should be the standardization of the English language.
1 2 3 4 5 One successful method for improving the learning capacity of speakers of Black English would be to replace their dialect with Standard English.

(Originally published in Orlando Taylor, "Teachers' Attitudes toward Black and Nonstandard English as Measured by the Language Attitude Scale," in *Language Attitudes: Current Trends and Prospects*, edited by Roger W. Shuy and Ralph W. Fasold. Washington, D.C.: Georgetown University Press, 1973.)

Bibliography

This bibliography limits itself to comprehensive texts which do not demand a specialized background in linguistics, texts which seem likely to be useful to English teachers.

Dialectical Differences

Bailey, Richard W., and Robinson, Jay L., eds. *Varieties of Present-Day English.* New York: Macmillan Publishing Co., 1973.
> This collection from several writers focuses first on varieties of English as they are spoken outside the United States, moves to the social dialects used within the United States, and concludes with attention to English in the classroom.

Clark, Virginia P.; Eschholz, Paul A.; and Rosa, Alfred F., eds. *Language: Introductory Readings.* 2d ed. New York: St. Martin's Press, 1977.
> Although there is some overlapping and duplication in purpose and content between this collection and those by Bailey and Robinson, and Williamson and Burke, the scope is broader. The reader can see sociolinguistic information and issues set in a context of other ways of studying language. Little of the material could be used directly in classrooms below college level, but secondary teachers could draw upon several articles for curriculum and activities.

Reed, Carroll E. *Dialects of American English.* Rev. ed. Amherst: The University of Massachusetts Press, 1977.
> In his introduction to this book, Raven I. McDavid, Jr. asserts that it is "a good first book for any reader who has just become aware of dialect variations." The information is scholarly; it is compactly presented; and the style is lucid.

"Students' Right to Their Own Language." *College Composition and Communication* (special issue), Fall 1974.
> In support of a resolution passed by constituent groups within NCTE, this pamphlet delineates underlying linguistic and pedagogical issues and offers in elaboration of these issues a 129-item annotated bibliography.

Williamson, Juanita V., and Burke, Virginia M., eds. *A Various Language: Perspectives on American Dialects.* New York: Holt, Rinehart and Winston, 1971.
> Containing more scholarly papers than the Bailey and Robinson volume, this collection provides much factual and interpretive

information about the dialects of English in America. The information might occasionally be directly useable in classrooms below college level, but its principal value is for background about methods of dialect study and about specific features of certain dialects.

Linguistics for the Layperson

Greenberg, Joseph H. *A New Invitation to Linguistics.* New York: Anchor Books, 1977.
> In this short book, the former president of the Linguistic Society of America explains some of the basic problems and concepts involved in the study of language, including both the code properties of human language and language in its social and cultural context.

Hall, Robert A. *Linguistics and Your Language.* 2d rev. ed. New York: Anchor Books, 1960.
> A linguist addresses a general audience in language that is not highly technical. He shows what the science of linguistics is and tries to reassure a reader who is assumed to be worried about "incorrect," "ungrammatical," and "corrupted" language.

Spelling: Principle and Variety

Emery, Donald W. *Variant Spellings in Modern American Dictionaries.* Rev. ed. Urbana, Ill.: National Council of Teachers of English, 1973.
> Based on page-by-page analysis and comparison of five widely used contemporary dictionaries, this monograph lists variant spellings for about 2400 words. It provides evidence that no single authority for "correct" spelling exists for many words.

Hall, Robert A. *Sound and Spelling in English.* New York: Chilton Books, 1961.
> After a compressed discussion of the linguistic terminology and principles involved in discerning sound and spelling relationships, the monograph suggests a "rational approach" to the learning of spelling.

Dialect Teaching Material

Frogner, Ellen A. *Using the* Language Inquiry *as a Teaching Device.* Washington, D.C.: Bureau of Research, Office of Education, U.S. Department of Health, Education, and Welfare, 1969.
> The *Language Inquiry* included in the Appendix of this book is contained in this pamphlet. In addition, the responses of ten linguists to each item are tallied, and there are suggestions for comparing these with the responses of students and teachers in follow-up activities.

Hess, Karen; Maxwell, John C.; and Long, Barbara K. *Dialects and Dialect Learning.* Urbana, Ill.: National Council of Teachers of English, 1974.

An inservice kit comprised of booklets, tape cassettes, and a leader's manual, this material emphasizes the systematic nature of major nonstandard dialects and helps teachers decide whether to teach standard English to nonstandard speakers.

McDavid, Raven I., Jr.; Muri, John T.; and McDavid, Virginia. *Americans Speaking.* Urbana, Ill.: National Council of Teachers of English, 1967.
   This recording (12″, 33-1/3 rpm) contains speech samples from six dialect areas in the United States in the 1960s. An accompanying booklet includes transcriptions of the speech and analysis of salient dialect features.

Pooley, Robert C. *The Teaching of English Usage.* 2d ed. Urbana, Ill.: National Council of Teachers of English, 1974.
   Reflecting linguistic knowledge of dialects, this book suggests pedagogical strategies for giving information about standard informal English in elementary, junior high, and senior high school classes.

Shuy, Roger W. *Discovering American Dialects.* Urbana, Ill.: National Council of Teachers of English, 1967.
   Useful for students and teachers, this pamphlet offers practical information about the characteristics of several regional and social dialects.

Attitudes toward Usage

Marckwardt, Albert H., and Walcott, Fred G. *Facts About Current English Usage.* New York: Appleton-Century, 1938.
   This is actually two books in one: the grammar portion of Leonard's "Current Usage in Grammar as Ranked by Linguists" (included in the Appendix of this book) and Marckwardt and Walcott's investigation of the actual use of the items surveyed by Leonard. Divided into "established," "disputable," and "illiterate," the items from the Leonard study provide examples which can be used in attitude inventories.

Mittins, W. H.; Salu, Mary; Edminson, Mary; and Coyne, Sheila. *Attitudes to English Usage.* London: Oxford University Press, 1970.
   The English Usage Questionnaire (included in the Appendix of this book) appears in this collection. While differences between American and British English make some items inappropriate for Americans, most items can be used for attitude inventories. The authors' detailed discussion of each item can provide the basis for group examination of assumptions.

Shuy, Roger W., and Fasold, Ralph W., eds. *Language Attitudes: Current Trends and Prospects.* Washington, D.C.: Georgetown University Press, 1973.
   A collection of papers reporting empirical research on attitudes toward language is contained here. While the methodologies may interest only researchers in language, the conclusions of the studies have implications for all English teachers.

The Change Process

Bennis, Warren G.; Benne, Kenneth D.; and Chin, Robert, eds. *The Planning of Change.* New York: Holt, Rinehart and Winston, 1976.

> Although many of the articles in this collection are addressed to change in business rather than educational organizations, the authors offer theories and strategies for teachers interested in implementing change.

Havelock, Ronald. *The Change Agent's Guide to Innovation in Education.* Englewood Cliffs, N.J.: Educational Technologies Publications, 1973.

> As the title suggests, this practical book focuses on the change agent as the link between status quo and desired change. Because it addresses itself to educational problems, it can be of special help to teachers.

Lippit, Ronald; Watson, Jeanne; and Westley, Bruce. *Dynamics of Planned Change.* New York: Harcourt Brace & Co., 1958.

> A good theoretical and practical overview of change is offered in this book.

Pfeiffer, J. William, and Jones, John E., eds. *A Handbook of Structured Experiences for Human Relations Training.* 5 vols. San Diego: University Associates, 1975.

————. *Annual Handbook for Group Facilitators.* San Diego: University Associates, 1976.

> Both the handbook and training volumes contain many practical suggestions for teachers interested in group process. Many of the exercises discussed in training volumes can be adapted to groups dealing with attitudes toward language.

Authors

Anne Ruggles Gere is Assistant Professor of English at the University of Washington and is Director of the Puget Sound Writing Program. She has taught English at the high school level and has conducted inservice programs for Seattle-area teachers. Editor of the Practice to Theory column in *English Journal,* she has published numerous articles in NCTE publications.

Eugene Smith is Associate Professor of English, University of Washington. In addition to eighteen years as a faculty member at Washington, he has taught in both elementary and secondary schools. He has also taught inservice courses for teachers and has been a curriculum consultant and a member of high school accreditation teams. Among his publications is the monograph *Teacher Preparation in Composition* (NCTE/ERIC, 1969).

WARNER MEMORIAL LIBRARY
EASTERN UNIVERSITY
ST. DAVIDS, PA 19087-3696